ERNIE

ERNIE

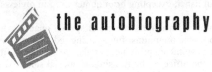

the autobiography

Ernest Borgnine

CITADEL PRESS
Kensington Publishing Corp.
www.kensingtonbooks.com

CITADEL PRESS BOOKS are published by

Kensington Publishing Corp.
850 Third Avenue
New York, NY 10022

All Kensington titles, imprints, and distributed lines are available at special quantity dis-counts for bulk purchases for sales promotions, premiums, fund-raising, educational, or institutional use. Special book excerpts or customized printings can also be created to fit specific needs. For details, write or phone the office of the Kensington special sales manag-er: Kensington Publishing Corp., 850 Third Avenue, New York, NY 10022, attn: Special Sales Department; phone: 1-800-221-2647.

CITADEL PRESS and the Citadel logo are Reg. U.S. Pat. & TM Off.

Photo Acknowledgments:

Tovern Productions
Orion Pictures Corporation
Metro-Goldwyn-Mayer Studios Inc.
Warner Entertainment, Inc.
20th Century-Fox

ISBN-13: 978-0-8065-2942-4
ISBN-10: 0-8065-2942-3

First Citadel hardcover printing: August 2008
First trade paperback edition: August 2009

10 9 8 7 6 5 4 3 2 1

Printed in the United States of America

Electronic edition:

ISBN-13: 978-0-8065-3150-2 (e-book)
ISBN-10: 0-8065-3150-9 (e-book)

To my beloved mother and father, Anna and Charles Borgnine.
To Mom, who encouraged me when she said, "Have you
thought of becoming an actor? You always like to make a fool of yourself
in front of people. Why don't you give acting a try?"

To Dad: You never stopped believing, even during the tough times
at the beginning. God bless you both.

Contents

Foreword

Ernest Borgnine is one of the Great Treasures of the entertainment world. He has done it all: Broadway, movies, television, stock. The whole works. And you can throw in an Academy Award! But I know him on a different level. A pal you can hang out with, play golf, go eat with, whatever. A best friend! A man who is passionate about life and is interested in just about everything you can think of and more than likely knows a lot about it. And when it comes to acting, well, you can forget that, he is the best.

He has done me a lot of favors and the most precious one is his friendship. He has sent me strange gifts and I in return to him. I have been trying to outgift him forever, but it is great to have a buddy that kinda thinks like you do.

But enough of this palaver. I could go on forever with all the things he has done for me, you, and just about everybody, but if I can steal a line from the movie, "What are you going to do tonight, Marty?" I'm going to read a great book. It's called *Ernie*.

—George Lindsey

Preface

It's Sunday night, January 13, 2008. Much to my delight, I've been nominated for a Golden Globe Award for my work in the Hallmark TV movie *A Grandpa for Christmas.*

I always get a little dreamy and reflective during awards ceremonies. Nominees always say, "Winning is nice, but it's a thrill just to be nominated." And outsiders think, *Yeah, yeah, sure. But you really want to win.*

Of course we do. However, it really *is* a thrill just to be nominated. Especially when you're my age (ninety-one). And to be acting, still, after nearly sixty years—that's a rare privilege.

So I'm sitting in my Beverly Hills home, the one I bought in 1965, watching the Golden Globes, looking at all the fresh young faces (to my eyes, sixty is fresh and young!), and thinking, *If I were starting out today, what kind of parts would I be playing?*

Given my size—five-foot-nine and hefty—chances are good I'd be offered roles like that big guy, the Thing, Michael Chiklis played in *Fantastic Four.* Or maybe that part John Travolta had in *Hairspray.* It's been a long time since I played a role in a dress or a toga. Not that anyone has a webpage calling for more of Ernie Borgnine's legs.

That's what's going through my mind as I'm tuned in to the Golden Globes. At the time—January 2008—the writer's strike was on and, as a result, the Golden Globe Awards ceremony has been stripped down to an hour-long special where the winners are simply announced and clips are shown from all the nominated movies and shows. However, I look at the bright side—it saved me the trouble of having to dry-clean my tux.

The presenters applaud as winners are announced, and my mind continues to drift. Please don't think I'm rude; I have to admit I don't know a lot of the winners or the shows and movies for which they're nominated. It's tough to keep up with all the channels, movies, and DVDs that are out there. When I started out there were three TV networks, no such thing as home video, and just a few studios making far fewer movies.

A reporter asked me earlier in the day, "Mr. Borgnine, do you have any plans to retire?"

I answered, "Retire to what? To work in the garden? Drive my beloved wife Tova crazy? (Or should that be 'crazier'?) Heck, no!"

A lot of what keeps me going is that old-fashioned work ethic I had pounded into me by my first-generation immigrant parents, bless them, when I was growing up in Connecticut.

Besides, I am an actor by profession and I love what I do.

Which brings me to this memoir. For years people have been telling me I should write my life story. I always respond, "I'm just a working stiff—who'd want to read about me?" That was my attitude for years.

When I became the oldest living actor to be nominated for a Golden Globe (not to mention being the oldest living actor to have won an Oscar), I had a change of heart. All modesty aside, why *shouldn't* I write my life story?

I've had quite a run. And since I can still remember most of it, I want to share some of my favorite stories and memories, and maybe give some tips to actors who are just starting out. See, I've made some great pictures, some good pictures, some not-so-good pictures, and a few out-and-out stinkers. (I have the distinction of appearing in more of the 100 Most Enjoyably Awful Movies of All Time as listed in Razzie Award–founder John Wilson's book *The Official Razzie Movie Guide* than any other actor—*The Adventurers* (1970), *The Legend of Lylah Clare* (1968), and *The Oscar* (1966), among them.

Well, they can't all be gems. But what fun they all were, and every one of them was a learning experience.

I've died onscreen almost thirty times. I've been shot, stabbed, kicked, punched through barroom doors by Spencer Tracy and Gary Cooper; pushed in front of moving subway trains, devoured by rats and a giant mutated fish; blown up in spaceships, melted down into a Technicolor puddle, jumped into a snake pit, and I perished from thirst in the Sahara Desert. I bounced around a capsized ocean liner, beat Frank Sinatra to death, impaled Lee Marvin with a pitchfork, and had my way with Raquel Welch.

Any one of those would've been worth the journey.

I've acted in westerns, comedies, war pictures, crime dramas, horror, science fiction, disaster films, and Biblical epics. I once played the head of a Viking clan. I've been bad guys, good guys, cops, crooks, murderers, mob bosses, western villains, and an Amish farmer. I've portrayed Asians, Jews, Italians (not much of a stretch), Irishmen, Swedes, and Mexicans.

Hell, I even played Satan once, in *The Devil's Rain*. It wasn't hard—I just channeled some of the agents I've had over the years.

I've sustained countless injuries over the years and even survived a plane crash. I've traveled all over the world for my work; stayed in five-star hotels in Europe and in bug-infested huts in South America. I've been blessed to have worked with some of the greatest writers and directors in film history and almost four generations of stars from Clark Gable and Joan Crawford and Bette Davis to Bart Simpson and Sponge-

Bob SquarePants. I've seen this business change technologically from the fuzzy photography of live TV to entire movies produced on computers.

I remember when a corned-beef sandwich at Nate 'n Al Delicatessen in Beverly Hills cost 85 cents. (I don't know how much they are now—corned beef is on my look-but-don't-touch list.) When I first came out here in 1952, a house in Beverly Hills went for $30,000; today that same house would go for $5 million. Movie admission was 35 cents; today it's $10 or even $11; a bag of popcorn was a dime. Today it's $5. Once the town made westerns like *Shane* and *The Searchers* and *The Magnificent Seven* and had larger-than-life leading men like Gable and Cooper, Bogart and Cagney, and the tall cowboy everyone called the Duke. Today, I see our so-called movie stars in *People* magazine and most of them look like they belong on the FBI's Most Wanted List wall at the post office, all tattoos and body piercings.

I started working at a time when a movie cost less than half a million dollars to produce. Now a movie that costs $50 million is considered low budget.

In these pages I'll show you what Hollywood was like more than half a century ago and how it's changed, sometimes for the better, sometimes for the worse.

So *grazie infinite* for stopping by. *Divertiti.*

ERNIE

 *Chapter 1*

In the Beginning . . .

One day in October 1950, while going from audition to audition, trying unsuccessfully to find a job, I was walking along Tenth Avenue grumbling to myself, "Dummy, why did you ever get into this business? You only work once a month, at best, because according to agents, 'People don't want to see your particular mug too much.'"

Well, I did not believe that. Movies were more than just pretty boys and leading men. Jimmy Cagney was not pretty. Neither was Eddie Robinson.

But I had a family and I needed work badly. If I couldn't find it in movies or on the stage, I'd have to find it somewhere else. As the horns of boats on the Hudson River reached my ears, I imagined myself working on a tug or loading cargo or just fishing for our dinner.

Suddenly I smelled hot chestnuts. Some vendor on the corner was selling them. It reminded me of my mother. When I was a youngster, she'd cut chestnuts, put them in a pan on top of the stove, and let them roast. The whole house would become permeated with that smell. It was wonderful. So I walked a little closer, not to buy any, because I didn't have any money, but just to smell.

Well, as fate would have it—and trust me, luck plays a big part in the life of any successful person—I saw a sign on that vendor's cart that became my philosophy. The sign read, "I don't want to set the world on fire, I just want to keep my nuts warm."

In other words, don't plan big. Go from step to step to step—forward. If you've got talent and perseverance, and fate is willing to lend an occasional hand, the rest will take care of itself.

Chapter 2

Welcome to America

My father was born Camillo Borgnino, in a little town called Ottiglio in northern Italy. Ottiglio is located above Toreno and is surrounded by mountains. Years later, when I first visited my ancestral home, I wondered why anyone would leave such a paradise.

America. It was the land of sky's-the-limit opportunity, and the Borgninos wanted to see how high they could reach. At that time, the family had enough money to send one member over. They decided to send the mother first, by steamer, to find a place to live and a job in the United States, where the others would ultimately follow. Can you imagine a woman in her twenties, leaving her kids and husband behind, heading to a new country where she didn't know the language (but learned it fast)? However, she was resourceful, thrifty, and young and the men decided to stay behind to keep working and saving money. It was the right choice. She headed to New Haven, the town where many Italians went.

Within a few months, her husband—my grandfather—came over on a freighter with their three sons: Joe, my dad, and Freddy.

My grandfather started working in the brickyard and so did the boys. Not after school, but instead of school. They had to in order to make enough money. My grandfather worked there until his death. He was a hardworking, very quiet man. He always sat at the head of the table. Even though it was round, everybody knew he was at the head. I think I subconsciously channeled him when I played Ragnar, the Viking leader, a man of few words and a big, scary sword.

Each night, at dinner, my grandfather doled out a glass of wine to each of his children and to his wife and drank the rest of the jug himself. He listened while the rest of the family discussed things, offering guidance when he thought it was necessary. The family grew by two in America: my Aunt Lenna, and my Aunt Louise. After graduating from school, Lenna became a successful stock and bond broker and Louise went to work as a Realtor for a company called Clark, Hall, and Peck

At some point, my aunts—who had their eye on high society—felt they were being looked down upon because they were Italian. So they changed their name to Borgnine. After that, everyone took us for French people who happened to eat a lot of pasta and garlic bread.

My grandparents made themselves a nice little home where I used to spend my summer vacations as a boy. They had a great big garden in the back where they grew all their own vegetables. Grandma used to put away all kinds of goodies for the winter and made her own bread, spaghetti, and macaroni. They lived quite nicely. They even made their own wine, just like in Ottiglio. Back then, there weren't any laws against it.

My dad, though—he was a restless one. He decided one day in the middle 1910s that he'd had enough of the brickyard and wanted to make his way to New York City and see what a big metropolis had to offer. He figured that, at the very least, it would offer bricklaying at a better hourly wage.

But dad didn't end up building walls. He found himself at the Waldorf-Astoria working as a waiter for the famous Oscar of the Waldorf. It wasn't until years later that he found out that Oscar had a last name and it was Tschirky. Obviously, it didn't hurt his career not having a French-sounding name!

Oscar took a liking to my father and he said, "You stick with me, kid, I'll make you a multimillionaire." My father laughed. He was a very good waiter and he might have made manager one day, but in the meantime, New York was a pretty expensive place even then, in the 1920s, and he couldn't support himself on seventy cents an hour plus tips. So like any young man in a hurry, he gave it up. Oscar was sorry to see him go. I think he was interested in having my father make some of the foods he had known in the Old Country.

Anyway, my father moved back to Connecticut and went back into making bricks. From there he matriculated to working on the railroad.

While the Borgninos were busy becoming Americans, my mother made a similar journey. She came from a little town called Carpi, just outside of Modena, Italy, with her sister. They came to a place called Centerville, which—as the name suggests—is the "center," in this case of a little town called Hamden, Connecticut. They didn't have very many motion pictures in those days, but they had dances. Everyone went, and that's where my father met my mother. They married a few months later and he moved in with her in Hamden.

A little over a year later, on January 24, 1917, I was born. I know I made two people happy. One was my sainted mother who, of course, didn't have to carry me anymore. I was a pretty big boy—no surprise there, about nine pounds. Even when I was on the outside of my mother, the poor lady had a rough time carrying me around. I don't think it would've helped if they had those slings that moms have today. I'd have tipped her over like a bear cub stuck in a tree.

My father was happy, too, of course, though he was torn: my arrival kept him from enlisting to fight in World War I. But he had a new family to support and that's what mattered to him most. I was touched and surprised when, years later, he confided to me, that not being able to serve is one of his few regrets.

"I wish to goodness I'd gone just to be able to know what it was all about."

Dad was like that. Patriotic to the bone over his new homeland, and able to embrace and grow from all experiences, even negative ones. That outlook also kept me going during the lean years.

Unfortunately, Dad was also the kind of a person who was easily enticed to roll the dice with the men and have a drink or two. Two years after I was born my mother got tired of not having enough money due to his drinking and gambling, so she packed me up and we took a train ride to Chicago. We didn't have the money for a Pullman sleeper, so we sat—and slept—in our seats for nearly two days.

The choice of Chicago was not as random as it seemed. First, it was far from the wagging tongues of Connecticut. Divorce was frowned on, and my mother didn't want to hear any of that. Second, I was suffering from mastoiditis, an inflammation of the ears that caused me a lot of pain and kept filling with—and leaking—fluids that made it tough for me to hear. She knew someone who knew someone who knew a doctor who was a specialist.

This doctor told her to immerse me in a bathtub filled with water as cold as she could make it, which meant a layer of ice cubes. Then she was supposed to drain the tub and put me in very hot water. So with pans and kettles whistling, I'd be frozen, then boiled. It didn't drain my ears, but it did crack the tub. I had the illness until I was about eighteen. To this day, I can't bear to be in water that is anything other than "warm." On the other hand, I had a lot of "damn cold" memories to draw on when I made *Ice Station Zebra.*

After a few months in Chicago, my mother took me to Italy to live. Her father was the well-to-do Count Boselli, who used to be the financial adviser to Victor Emmanuel, the King of Italy. I remember my grandfather's farm. He had a big baronial estate. It even had its own church. I loved working on the farm with the farmers and riding the oxen they called "Bo."

In the fall they slaughtered the pigs, which consisted of hitting them on the head and cutting their throats. It was actually quite merciful. They'd always take the bladder of one, blow it up, and make a kind of football out of it. We played some bruising games with those bladders, enjoying the kind of camaraderie you just don't find outside a rustic village. Today, people have much less interaction. It's a shame. I learned a lot about life from those farmers, especially the idea that if you work together, without ego—whatever you're doing—the end result is a lot richer. Not surprisingly, the movies I made that turned out best had that kind of mutual support on the set.

It was enchanting in Italy except for going to religious schools. Nuns can be awfully nice people, but they're not all Julie Andrews. They're strict. Some of them were just plain mean. I sure caught my share of their discipline. I used to go home with my hands swollen from being beaten. My mother would ask me, "Why are you such a bad boy?"

I'd say, "I'm not bad. But if I ask a question too loud or at the wrong time or drop a book, they come along and swat me."

"Just remember," she said, not wanting to criticize the nuns, "God knows the truth."

I was okay with that. When I face Saint Peter, I'm betting he'll wink and let me pass.

Naturally, we went to our little church on the estate every Sunday. With my mother there, I felt safe from the nuns. After Mass, while we were waiting for Sunday dinner to be prepared, my uncle used to take me on the barge that went across the river. Despite my fear of the cold water, I enjoyed those trips. It's funny, now, to think about how I had ridden almost all the forms of transportation known to man at the time. I'd been on a boat, a train, an early motorcar, a horse, and an ox. All I was missing was a trip on a biplane, which would occasionally pass overhead to our great excitement. Back then, you could actually get your arms around much of what the world had to offer.

Talking about change, I went back there recently and saw the river I used to cross. They have a bridge there now. You can cross quickly and easily by foot or car. It's faster, but not necessarily better.

I loved watching my grandfather go to work in the morning. He had his own carriage and horse and he was driven by a coachman. He would sit in the backseat with his long cutaway coat, his top hat, cane, and even spats. Everybody bowed to him as he passed, and he bowed back

"*Buon giorno, buon giorno,* how are you, how are you?" he would reply with a gracious wave of his hand.

My grandfather died before Mussolini took over and the king became nothing but a figurehead. The new regime's changes trickled down to our family as well. Except for the farmhands, all the people that used to respect him, and us, were now rude and impatient whenever we went to town.

"Come on, get out of the way, you're bothering us," they'd say as they tried to ride their horses or carts past our carriage. And the indignities didn't stop there. The local government took my family's land and most of their possessions. My mother and grandmother ended up in the little town of Carpi. My mother had a little coffee shop and sold drinks on the side to customers who had hangovers.

To me, though, the move was a new adventure. I missed the farm and the farmhands, but now I had all of Carpi as my backyard along with kids my own age. I remember as a boy I used to go to the coffee shop and stuff candy in my clothes. Then I would hide underneath my grandmother's big bed. Looking out, I'd see my mother and my grandmother walk into the room. Knowing exactly where I was, they'd say to each other, "I wonder where that little bad boy went," and there I'd be eating candy and thinking I'd fooled them—again and again. I'd finally pop out from underneath. My grandmother always laughed and hugged me. You would never guess, from her quick smile and gentle eyes, how much she had lost to the new regime.

She died when I was about six years old. She had a huge funeral. People didn't come to the funeral because she was nobility and they felt obligated. They came because she was a great lady who had earned the love and respect of her community.

Chapter 3

Back Home

All the time we were in Italy my father had been writing to my mother. "Please come home, please come home," he'd write at least once a week. He even sent a record for the Victrola with lyrics that went, "My son, my son, my boy, my boy."

My dad was persistent.

After a few years my mother broke down. They did love each other, and my father said he had settled down and gotten a good job and they'd live nicely. Also, once again, my poor health contributed to a move. I'd managed to come down with malaria, which was almost epidemic in coastal regions of Italy in the early 1920s. The doctors told my mother that the moist climate wasn't good for me and I should be taken somewhere else. Connecticut seemed a good bet.

In 1923, we came back on a ship called the *Dante Alighieri*, which was named after the famed Italian poet, of course. Dante wrote about hell. During my passage to America, I got a taste of what that was like. The very first morning at sea my mother dressed me up in these Lord Fauntleroy clothes with a little flowing tie and a knickers suit, all hand knitted. She told me where to wait for her in the dining room and she'd be right there. I got strange looks from some of the more rough-and-tumble kids who were traveling third class, but that wasn't the worst of it.

When I walked up this passageway I suddenly felt the ungodliest thing in my life: my stomach seemed to be knocking up against my tongue. I was immensely seasick, so I just dashed into the first room I could find. I lay on my back and in the dim light I looked up and saw this man's face in the bunk above. He looked like Lon Chaney in makeup. And I'd woken him. I was frightened, but I was just too sick to move.

In the meantime, my mother went to the dining room expecting to see me.

"Where's my boy, where's my boy?" she said with increasing alarm. She began to shout that I had gone overboard.

Well, that mean-looking man had heard the commotion and, slipping from his bunk, he scooped me in his arms and took me into the bright daylight. He followed the shouting and reunited me with my mother.

My mother was so glad to see me she hugged me and hit me at the same time. I was still sick and finally threw up. My mother didn't care. She was actually on the way back to the cabin where she had a pistol and was intending to shoot herself, convinced she had lost me.

My second punishment during the passage came when we were coming into New York Harbor. Everyone was gathered at the railing, watching as we passed the Statue of Liberty. Except me. There was a sandbox on deck, and I noticed that there was no one in it. So I went over and started to play. No sooner had I picked up a little wooden shovel than my mother grabbed my ear—so hard, in fact, that we could have skipped the hot-cold treatments to drain my ears and just had her yank them. She dragged me to the bow, put me at attention, and slapped me on the backside.

"When you see that lady, you stand at attention," she commanded.

I've been standing at attention for this country ever since, believe me.

Chapter 4

Connecticut Memories

It's a weird thing to look at your father and see a stranger. He seemed vaguely familiar and yet he wasn't familiar at all. And it wasn't as if I could see my features in his. I was only seven and my face was that of a boy. This was a man with a hint of red hair and a stern look about him. He obviously recognized me, though, because he came over and hugged me with the big hull of the ship behind me. The smell of brick dust on him kicked the smell of the sea out of my nose. We claimed our big trunk and made our way crosstown to Grand Central Station. The noise and smoke and crowds of the city were startling after years spent on the farm and then on Carpi. But it was also energizing and my eyes darted everywhere, taking it all in. Especially Times Square, which we passed through on the way to the train station. The marquees of the theaters, the bulbs and neon of the signs, the big billboards advertising more movies than I'd seen in my entire life, were hypnotic. That wasn't when the acting bug bit me, but I sure felt the beating of its little wings.

Except for the clothes on my back and the memories in my head, I hadn't brought anything of the old country with me. But that was okay. My mother said that this was going to be a new start.

"Another one," she added wistfully.

We returned to North Haven, where my Dad was true to his word. He had settled down and my parents were very happy together. A year after our return my mother had a daughter, Evelyn June Borgnine, born on April 25th. It was quite an exciting event for me not because I had a sister—that hadn't hit me yet—but because I had the chance to place telephone calls to my aunts and my grandmother, who lived nearby, to tell them the news. Even the operator sensed the excitement in my voice and wanted to know what was up. I told her. She didn't know me from General Pershing, but she congratulated me just the same.

My baby sister and I became great friends. She trusted me to look out for her, in the school yard, at picnics, at the movies, wherever we went. And I did. Except for once, which I'll get to in a bit.

Everything was fine for a while. In fact, the only problem was school. When we first got back, my mother sent me to classes with those Lord Fauntleroy clothes. I walked onto the school grounds and saw these kids rolling down a hill inside a tire hoop and went over to see if I could play, too. They looked at me and, like they had a single brain thinking the same thought, one of the kids said, "Would you like to roll down the hill?"

The other boys all nodded.

I said, "Yes, yes, *mio amico*, I'd like to go, sure." I snuggled into the narrow rubber ring, but instead of rolling me the way they had gone, they turned me around and shoved me over the other side. Not only was it a rockier road, which knocked my insides around, but when I reached the bottom the tire fell to its side and I landed in the biggest puddle you ever saw. I never went to school that first day. I went home, filthy and soaked, and my mother let me have three swats across the backside for being such a sap.

The next day I went back to school and acted like nothing happened. Actually, I'm not sure the kids even recognized me. My poufy outfit was all dirty, so I wore overalls and a button-down shirt.

I wouldn't say I was the best student in the world. Mathematics eluded me. I did not like the regimentation of it, I think. A plus B equals C. There was no room for the imagination. I guess that was why I liked history and geography. I liked thinking about different times and places and picturing myself in them. Not quite the acting bug yet, but another glimpse of those wings batting by! I also liked English, especially spelling. I liked comparing those words to the Italian words I knew. They made me feel richer, somehow.

I had only been in that school two semesters when the Depression hit and we had to move. We relocated to rooms in Hamden where there was more work, and then to New Haven when a house became available for rent. It was located on Cherry Ann Street and was owned by the City or the bank, possibly a foreclosure. All I know is that we paid $15.00 a month for it. Can you imagine: an entire house for the cost of a movie ticket nowadays. Talk about change!

My father, God bless him, was always out hustling and always found work. The lessons of Oscar of the Waldorf were not lost on him. He was always trying harder, pushing, and he always ended up as one of the bosses, whatever job he was on. When the WPA came to town, he really managed to prosper.

WPA stood for Works Progress Administration, which was government money building things to keep people employed. My father was a foreman on various roads and bridges that were built in New Haven. Those structures are still standing, today. Even at the age of thirteen I thought the WPA was a wonderful idea. I don't understand why we can't do that today.

We had a bigger and bigger garden every year because Mom wanted to grow corn and tomatoes and flowers for the table. So every day in springtime, before we went to school and work, my father and I would get outside and spade the ground. I loved that work, not just because it was something my Dad and I did together, but because I could see the results as the garden grew. If you've never eaten something you helped to grow, you should try it. Nothing on earth will ever taste better than a carrot you raised from a seed. In fact, many days I'd run home from school to work the soil. You'd never believe it to look at me now, but in those days I got pretty lean from all the running and hoeing. In fact, it was so satisfying that when summertime came around I got work on a local farm owned by wonderful people called Mantovani. I made some money and stayed out of mischief and learned on my own what my father had always talked about: the work ethic. It made me feel good inside and out. And best of all, there were times when I caught a smell or saw a bag of seed and it whisked me back to the farm in Italy. Yes, people and places are different the world over. But most things, the basics, are the same.

Speaking of the world, we had a kind of mini-world in our own backyard. There were a bunch of kids on Cherry Ann Street. We had Poles, we had blacks, we had Italians, we had Irish, we had just about every nationality there was. We all used to congregate under a big streetlight in front of the Yardleys'. I think they were more afraid of what a bunch of young teens might do than what we did do, which was mostly playing hide-and-seek or thinking of a way to get to the Long Island Sound for a swim. We also liked to race, from corner to corner or around the block. I loved the sound and feel of the wind rushing by my ears. Like tilling the earth, there was something primal about it—like I was a lion or an ancient hunter.

More early acting? You bet!

When enough of us got together we played baseball, we played football, we played everything except basketball. In those days it was considered a rather sissy game because after you sank a basket you walked away from the key and got back in line to do it again. It wasn't anything like it is today, running around full-court. Besides, girls played it too, standing flat-footed in front of the hoop and throwing the ball from between their knees in an underhand toss.

I never dated in my teenage years. For one thing, I rarely had enough money. I gave everything I earned to my parents. Also, I was too shy. You wouldn't think so, because I was around my mother and sister and aunts and cousins all the time. But they didn't look at me the way some of those other girls did. In fact, they didn't *look* like some of those girls did! They caused strange stirrings that I didn't understand. So I hung with the guys at a time when hanging with the guys meant nothing more than they were your buddies.

Holidays in our home were always my favorite time of year. The big ones were the Fourth of July, when we got together with family and neighbors—even the Yardleys—and celebrated our great nation. I also remember Armistice Day—now Veterans Day—which was a little more solemn, when we honored our war heroes. And, of course there were my favorites: Christmas and Easter.

Money was usually pretty tight, so Christmas was a time of homemade gifts. Except one year, when some guy came along with $14.00 that he owed my father. I was lucky enough to be the one who answered the door and pocketed the money. On Christmas morning I got out of bed very early, stole downstairs with two of my socks. I put $7.00 in one sock for my parents and $7.00 in the other for my sister and myself. Then I went upstairs and said to my parents, "Look! Santa Claus came!" My mother and father were crying, they were so happy. I never did find out what happened to that man, though. If my Dad ever found out where the money came from, he never let on to me.

I'll never forget when I got my first pair of good pants for Easter. I was fifteen or sixteen. When we got back from the clothing store I laid them across the bed and just looked at them, and said, "Boy, that's a far cry from knickers." I felt like a real gentleman, like a country squire back in Italy.

It was the first time I felt like a man. And *that* wasn't acting!

I also liked Mother's Day, when I'd bring Mom a great big bunch of flowers. I always told her I'd picked them in the woods. I didn't dare tell her that I got them from the cemetery. It may not have been kosher, but I felt my mother would enjoy them more than the deceased did.

In those days, my best buddy was a kid named Joey Simone. He was much shorter than me and my mother used to call us Mutt and Jeff, after the newspaper comic strip about two friends, one very tall and one very short.

Joey was a young Italian boy whose family was from Sicily. They always spoke with a wonderful, thick Italian accent, a dialect of the Bareza region that had been their home. The mother and dad always used to work on a farm and you'd often see them in the fields hauling around these big bundles of grass they used to feed the animals. They worked hard, but they were always smiling. They seemed genuinely happy to be working together.

Mrs. Simone was amazing. When she came home each night, around 6:30, she would not only prepare dinner but also do the wash—by hand. You always knew when she was doing that because you'd hear her singing. In fact, when I think back, my youth was filled with the sounds of community. Her folk songs, the mixture of different languages on the street corners, the sounds of chickens some of the residents kept in pens. Kids growing up today don't have those sounds. They shut them out with cell phones and iPods. I think they're missing something, a sense of roots and heritage, warm memories they would treasure in their older years. It's too bad, really.

Mrs. Simone made a lot of pizza. That's how pizza got started: with moms who had dough left over from making bread. They'd roll it out and spread some tomato sauce on top with some salami and mushrooms or whatever they had there, and heat it for dinner. Today, people like Mrs. Simone, making homemade pies, would be wealthy! Maybe she should have gone to New York and worked with Oscar.

My favorite activity was hiking on Pine Rock Mountain. Joey and I felt like explorers, picking among the boulders and thistles. You didn't worry about Lyme disease back then. If a tick bit you, you burned it off with a cigarette or hot match. If you got poison ivy, you washed and scratched.

We used to go everywhere together. We'd go swimming, always bare, at Martha's Hole and Ear Hole and all kinds of places. Back then nobody thought anything of boys skinny-dipping. We didn't go in the lake—which was actually some kind of quarry that had filled with water—because too many people had drowned there. If you threw something in you couldn't see it hit bottom. It was that deep.

We also used to go to Farnham's Farm to steal apples and vegetables we couldn't grow. We didn't do it to be mean but to help our folks. The more we ate there, the less we had to eat at home. I'd always tell my mother "I ate at Joey's," and he'd tell his Mom he ate at my place. Fortunately, Mr. Farnham never caught us. I don't know what story we would have told him. He was always busy with a big stone crusher he owned. It kept grinding rock that was hauled from Pine Rock Mountain. The stone was used to make roadbeds and such. Maybe it was Mr. Farnham, or maybe I just got bigger, but when I went back to my old home Pine Lock seemed more like a hill than a mountain.

One night, we went looking for celery because we wanted something to munch on. We were crossing the Beaverdale Cemetery when we came to a big hedge that separated the graveyard from a large garden. As we started to go through it, up popped several heads. We ran like the dickens.

"Hey, where you going?" hissed a voice.

It was three of our buddies who had just finished searching for potatoes in the same garden. It was crook meeting crook. Since they were already over there, they grabbed a few stalks for us. They weren't just being nice; they liked the danger.

Joey and I also knew a spot where bakery trucks would drop off cartons of two-day-old bread they couldn't sell anymore. They left it outside the bakery where, I suppose, it was going to be ground into bread crumbs or croutons or some such. We always took as many of those boxes as we could carry. Sometimes more, hiding some of them and then going back. The first time I brought it home, my mother asked, "Where did you get all this stuff?"

I told her and she worked some wonders with it to freshen it up—

putting it in the oven with water, remoisturizing it—and it tasted just fine.

I started seeing less and less of Joey as we grew older, since he had to work with his mother and father so they could save money and buy a house. Occasionally, when I had the time, I would help them out. My buddy Joey Simone had gone into business selling fish and chips. He had a little store of his own and also brought his products to factories to sell. I remember one day Joey and I were rattling along in his truck. You could hear every bolt and piston and spring in that thing—*boom, bidda boom, ping, bang.*

I said, "My God, doesn't this thing drive you crazy?"

Joey said, "No, I just turn up the radio a little louder."

Now that I think of it, maybe Joey was the forefather of the iPod generation!

Chapter 5

A Little Family History

North Haven, Connecticut, was our family town. That's where my parents and their siblings stayed and had children. My Uncle Freddie became a good mechanic. My father was a jack-of-all-trades. My Uncle Joe ran a steam shovel for the International Silver Company in Meriden, Connecticut. To paraphrase Dickens, it was the best of times . . . and also had some of my worst times.

When I was still a young man, my mother started having delusions that everybody was against her. She didn't recognize family members from time to time. We understand this illness today; back then, we called it senility, even though she was only in her late fifties.

I think the worst of it was at the very beginning, when I didn't know she was sick. My mother told me about my sister coming in late, that she must be running around like a whore.

I said, "Mom, you're wrong. Evie has a job. She isn't doing what you think."

My mother would get angry and say, "No, no, believe me! I know what's happening. I know what's going on. She smoking, she's running around."

Well, I didn't know what to do. My mother was *so* certain. When my sister came home that night—my father was still at work—I faced her. I repeated what our mother had said.

"She's lying!" my sister said.

Hearing those words triggered something in me and—I'm ashamed, now, to say it—but I hit my sister. I really gave it to her, bad, slapping her around.

She cried "No, no, Ernie. I'm not a whore! Mom is wrong—she's sick!"

That was the first time anyone had dared to say that, but some part of me knew it must be true. My sister was a good person. I felt sick about what I'd done and I held her close and begged her forgiveness—not just then, but many times since. She forgave me at once; she's that kind of woman, generous to her bones.

That was the beginning of a long decline for my poor Mom. I can't account for the onset of her illness at such a young age. I do know that her life had not been easy since our return to America. In addition to the hardships of the Depression and watching out that my Dad didn't slip back into his old ways—his resolve was strong, but he was still only human—she had experienced great tragedies in her family.

Before we had gone to Chicago, Mom's younger sister had married a gentleman in Hamden. I never knew his name. It was one of those situations back then when you had to get married. They had twins and then one more child. My mother worried openly to my Dad, at the time, that this was going to be a bad marriage and that something terrible would happen all through this family. She spoke of it almost like a curse was put on us. At the time, I had no idea what she meant, only that her voice and expression scared me.

Sure enough, the man that my mother's sister married became violent, abusive, a real lunatic, and was put away by the courts. Feeling alone and hopeless, my aunt took her youngest child and committed suicide under a train. We had just returned to America and her two lovely, orphaned twins were left in the care of my mother.

One day, when they were about five, the twins wanted to go down and watch people ice-skate. My mother bundled them up nicely, gave them money to buy a snack on the way, and off they went. But there were no skaters to watch and, disappointed, they went onto the pond to skate themselves. The reason there were no skaters is that the ice was too thin, and they fell through. With nobody there to rescue them, they both drowned.

That tragedy weighed on my mother's mind for the rest of her life. Shortly after the accident Mom came down with tuberculosis. She went to a Dr. Pakosta, a chiropractor, who was the only medical man we know. He actually kept her alive for a long, long time. But she was getting worse. She finally went to a doctor at New Haven hospital, a Dr. Posa. He told her she should pack up and go to somewhere warm like New Mexico or Arizona. Of course, she wouldn't leave her family. She continued to work as hard as ever, on her garden, keeping the house white-glove clean, making sure her children were well cared for. She was sick on-and-off for sixteen years, her mental state deteriorating for a year or two before she finally passed away.

During that time, I often stayed with my Uncle Joe so that Mom would have one less person to look after. I remember my dad saying "Your Mom and I love you very much, but she's sick and she's got to have rest. She can't take care of you the way that she wants to."

I used to sleep in Uncle Joe's attic, which I shared with a mouser that loved to cuddle alongside of me. Sometimes I'd find the cat asleep on top of my covers. One morning my Uncle Joe came to wake me and the place stunk to high heaven. You'd swear to God it was a skunk.

He said, "You peed the bed!"

Well, usually when you pee the bed it goes down. This was straight up. And my pajamas weren't even wet. It didn't make sense and I tried to explain that to him.

I said, "It must have been the cat!" But I couldn't convince him and I got the reputation for being a thirteen-year-old bed wetter! I look back at it now and laugh, but it wasn't a funny thing then because I had to go to the washtub and scrub everything till it was spotless and fresh-smelling.

One of the things that gave my mother a lot of pleasure during her waning years was her pet canary, Petie. She used to pull all the shades down and let the bird fly loose in the house. The canary would flit here and there and she just loved the sound of it. Unlike the cat, it always went back to the cage to do its business.

Anyway, one day the circus came to town and I was out bright and early. We used to earn some money in those days by helping to set up the grandstand seats under the seasoned eyes of the full-time roustabouts. I confess that more than once I thought about joining the circus and seeing the countryside. Does anyone do that anymore? I doubt it. Kids run away to the mall.

We carried all those heavy boards and, as in the old days on the farm, I was reminded about the importance of teamwork. When we were finished, we'd get two bits or so and free tickets to the afternoon show—never the sold-out evening performances.

I rushed home after doing all that hard work. I was tired, but I wanted to clean up real fast so I could get back and see the show. As I ran up the three steps leading to the porch, I could see my mother in the parlor, rocking back and forth on her chair. What I didn't see was Petie hanging on the screen door looking out. As I hit the door and flung it in I heard a shrill, terrible "re-e-e-t."

My mother jumped from the chair and screamed, "Petie!"

Without realizing it, I had dislodged her poor little bird and then stepped on it. I did not go to the circus that day. Maybe I should have blamed that on the cat, too.

One of the other activities that helped me become a man and reinforced the notion of teamwork was joining the Boy Scouts. I almost missed the boat on that one because—I kid you not—they couldn't find a shirt that fit me. I only had a shirt that *looked* like a Boy Scout shirt, something my mother found and dyed. So I put my insignias on that and they let me get by with it. Joey joined, too, reinforcing the bond we felt.

I had thick fingers and I had a hard time making knots. Eventually, though, I got the hang of it. Score one for determination, another valuable life lesson.

I did pretty well in scouting. I was just one merit badge short of becoming an Eagle Scout. More than anything in my formative years, scouting taught me how to be a man—self-sufficient and observant. I used to pay very close attention to what the scout leaders told us about the stars, about nature, about survival. I learned how to make a fire by rubbing sticks together, I learned how to cook food in the wild and how to make a crude lean-to as shelter. After a year or so I became the Assistant Scoutmaster of the troop at St. Anne's Church. It was wonderful. I'd take the new kids on twenty-mile hikes and share everything I'd been taught.

Scouting also changed my life in one very significant way. It happened when the Boy Scout circus came to town, the year after I had accidentally flattened poor Petie. My troop then, Longhouse Troop No. 12, was asked to participate as circus clowns. I came up with a different idea. I put on my father's long winter underwear with a smudge of mustard on the backside. I had a big bottle and a bib around my neck and I ran around like a little baby, wailing, "I want my Momma!"

Well, when I did that in the center ring, it brought down the house. The next year they insisted that we do it again. This time, though, I changed the act. I sat in the lap of John Murphy, the mayor of New Haven, something I would never have done as "myself." But with that cap and all, I was a baby and could do just about anything or sit anywhere I wanted. When I did my act he was engulfed with laughter. It was a big thing for New Haven.

And, yes. *That* was where the idea of being an actor—for real—first occurred to me. It was my first time doing something in front of people. In fact, I enjoyed it so much it helped me pick up my school grades. See, my teachers told me that if I raised my marks and proved I could handle some extracurricular activities, they would let me act in the class play at the end of the school year. I studied hard, joined the debating club, and landed a role in the play.

I honestly don't remember the name of the play. All I remember is that I was given the part of a Chinese kid. I went out on my own and found these little braids that looked like the ones worn by Chinese people I'd seen in a picture book, then I found a hat and everything else. I used a singsong voice onstage. It brought down the house. Afterward, a teacher came to me and said, "You are so good! You should become an actor."

I remember thinking, "Are you crazy? That's no way to make a living."

I guess I wasn't as smart as I thought.

Chapter 6

Borgnine's Navy

When I graduated from high school my mother, bless her, wanted me to be a barber. She felt it would provide me with steady work. I didn't care for the idea myself, but that didn't matter.

"You're going to barber school," she insisted.

It wasn't a school, as such: it was just a barbershop and all I did for about four or five days was clean up hair around the barber's chair. On the sixth day, I decided to hand in my broom. My mother wasn't happy. My Dad came to my rescue. He knew someone—his name was Sal. I never got to know his last name. He owned a vegetable truck. He figured it would be steady since lots of people had farms in the area and lots of people in nearby communities needed produce.

I wasn't too crazy about that idea, either, but my father made the deal.

Dad said, "He'll give you $3.00 a week and all the bananas and apples you can eat."

At 3:30 in the morning we'd make the rounds collecting produce, then go up and down streets for fourteen or fifteen hours, hawking radishes and bananas and everything else you could think of. Evidently,

Sal knew quite a few housewives along the way because there were times he'd just spend hours in their homes. I'd be sitting there in the truck. People would come up and want to buy something.

The net result of these two jobs was that I didn't want to become a barber or drive a truck. But the vegetable business did point me in my next direction. One day while I was working on the vegetable truck I noticed a sign that said JOIN THE NAVY, SEE THE WORLD. Remembering what my Dad had said about feeling he had missed something by not being in the service, I went to the navy recruiting office to investigate.

The recruiter said, "Did you pass high school?"

"Yes, sir."

He said, "You look in good shape. We'll give you a physical and be in touch."

The next day I got a call.

"Okay, kid," the caller said, "you passed."

"I passed—what?" I asked.

He said, "You're gonna be in the navy, son."

I figured I'd better talk to my folks before I was sworn in. I don't think they could have changed my mind, but I did want their blessings.

My heart was drumming like Mr. Farnham's rock crusher. I said, "Mom, guess what? I'm going to start working tomorrow for the government."

She said, "What government?"

I said, "Uncle Sam's. I just became a sailor."

Her face fell. She had such ambitions for this boy of hers, and now he was going to be a sailor, which meant that I was to go away and God alone knew what would happen to me. She had all the natural trepidations of a mother. My father's reaction was very different.

He said, "Son, you're not going to be tied to your mother's apron strings anymore and you're going to find out what this world is all about. I envy you this adventure you're about to have."

He talked to my mother and calmed her fears. The next morning he and I kissed each other and off he went to work. I kissed my Mom and off I went to the navy.

It was 1935 and I took a bus, along with other guys, to the Newport Training Station in Newport, Rhode Island. I was promptly given a haircut, uniforms, and a lesson: fall asleep hard and sleep deep when you can. Otherwise, your butt *will* drag.

We slept in hammocks in those days. They were tough to get used to, but even tougher was learning just to get into a hammock. You were up a good four feet and you had to learn how to dip it with your butt and kind of hurl yourself in sideways, up and over. And once in it, you had to learn how to balance yourself. Every now and then you could hear somebody fall out with a great thud. You could hurt yourself badly that way. Some guys ended up with broken arms. And there was nothing quite like being rocked to sleep in a pitching sea. You didn't only go from side to side but back to front and sometimes in little circles.

My hammock skills were pretty solid from the get-go, and my hammock-tying skills were even better. A superior officer was watching one day as I tied the lines after the hammocks were washed. He said, "What are you, a Boy Scout or something?"

I said, "Yes, sir." For me, it was just another reminder of lessons you learned one place being applied someplace else.

I was homesick at first, but that was soon taken out of me by the press of duties and things I had to learn. I don't know why, but 5:30 was the time they woke us all up. You had to dress, scrub your teeth, make up your hammock, then get to the real work. You had to learn the arms manuals and the right way to present arms and parade. You also had to learn how to use a bucket of water very sparingly. In boot camp, you had all the water you needed. When you got aboard ship, it would be an altogether different matter.

I spent all my free time studying and learning my blue jackets' manual. You learned a lot of things that I'd already picked up as a kid, like discipline. You had to have discipline in order to make things run right. It was wonderful to feel myself growing up.

After about two or three weeks of boot camp, they allowed the parents to visit. I was washing clothes and hanging them with these little ribbon-like ties when my Mom and Dad arrived.

A fellow recruit ran up. "Borgnine, your folks are here. Report front and center."

My mother and father had brought my two aunts and my sister Evelyn to see me. God, it was good to see them all and their big smiles—the biggest I'd ever seen—told me they felt the same. We spent a couple of hours together. I showed them around and they were very impressed. My mother saw the change in me and said so. My dad just smiled proudly, especially after I showed him how I handled a rifle.

That evening, I was on guard in front of B Barracks. I was walking along thinking how nice it had been for everyone to visit. I guess I was a little distracted. Suddenly, I saw somebody coming down the hill from the War College. I said to myself, "I'll say, halt, who goes there?" And as I was thinking that, I heard a voice say, "Come on, son. Say, 'Halt, who goes there?'"

I said stupidly, "Come on son, say halt who goes there?"

The response shivered my timbers from toe to chin. He said, "The captain of the base."

I didn't know whether to present arms or salute, throw the rifle around ceremoniously or throw it away.

I did none of those things. I just stood there, attentive as a sentry should be. The captain eyed me up and down and, apparently satisfied that I was sober and alert, he strode away.

I was lucky, that time. I never let myself daydream again while I was on duty.

I tried to be a good sailor, and evidently I did all right. They put me on a squad that had a boxing team. I'd never fought in a ring. I'd fought with the kids in the street or in the yard, but never with gloves on. The first time I got up on the canvas to get the feel of things I was scared stiff. I didn't know what to do.

This chief machinist mate was our instructor. He said, "Easy does it, kid. Just keep your arms up, try to block incoming punches when you can. Don't think about it, just do it."

I must have done something right because I knocked the guy out in four swings. He went down and started to turn white, with blood pouring from his nose and ears. It frightened the devil out of me and I never got back in the ring. Ironically, twenty years later, I'd make a movie called *From Here to Eternity* in which Monty Clift refused to box after killing a man in the ring. Let me tell you, I really felt for the character he was playing.

Chapter 7

Adventures at Sea

When I finished boot camp, I shipped out on the *Chaumont*, a double-ended son of a gun that navigated through the Panama Canal and on to the Pacific Coast. They worked us hard the whole trip.

The first time that I got off the *Chaumont* was in Balboa in Panama. I found I was walking funny and I wondered aloud, "What the heck's wrong with me?"

A shipmate said, "That's because of the wave motion at sea."

My legs still thought we were at sea and I was walking like I would onboard ship. It was the funniest sensation. The second thing someone said to me after reaching port was, "Hey, kid, you ever been with a woman?"

"Oh sure," I lied. I had never been with any girl.

Back in Connecticut, I was always afraid to approach the fairer sex. For one thing, I didn't know what the devil to talk to them about. I only knew the women in my family, and mostly what we talked about was family business. There was no get-to-know-you small talk. Being an average kid, there were times I felt like putting my arm around a girl and wondering what it would feel like. But, heck, that was just too terrifying to contemplate. What if she screamed? What if she didn't like me? What if she *did* like me and wanted more? My mother and grand-mother had taught me to respect all women. My very confused desires left me pretty much paralyzed.

Clearly, my fellow sailor had no such reservations. He said, "Let's get a whore."

I said, "Okay, let's go." I figured, What did I have to lose other than my virginity?

Then he said, "You take this here with you and when it's your turn you have to put that on."

I looked at the little square envelope he'd handed me. I had seen condoms one time in my father's drawer, stacked in a little plastic container. But I didn't know what they were for.

"Yeah, okay," I replied. "Thanks."

We walked over to a wooden shack with a corrugated tin roof. As I waited outside I heard grunts and groans. After they quieted, the girl came out and looked at me and said, "You're next, sailor."

I stuttered, "Okay, sure, I'm coming," and a few other inanities.

We went in and she was all business. Time is money, as the saying goes. She told me to leave the money on the counter—it was five bucks—then said, "Come on, pull down your pants and let's go." I opened my trousers, suddenly realizing that this is where the thing in the envelope went. It was rolled up tight and I started to stretch it out. I thought you had to put it on like a boot.

She looked at me and said, "You're kind of a greenhorn, huh, sailor?" She laughed and I was mortified, but she put it on for me. The minute she did, bam! it was over.

When I came out, my buddy looked over his cigarette and said "How was it?"

I told him it was great. And it was. I'd even gotten to see the girl's breasts, which was as undressed as she'd gotten before I finished.

"Well, listen," he went on. "We got to go get some Salvarsan, then take a shower and get cleaned up."

I had no idea what Salvarsan was, but we went down to the gym at the YMCA and took a pill. Then we went back to the ship, reported to the officer on deck that we had been with a whore and were told to take another Salvarsan. The pharmacist told me why, and I admit being a little shocked hearing that I'd been exposed to syphilis. The guys kidded me for months.

"Boy, you're going to get it now, you're going to get the clap."

I lived in dread for months until I finally woke up and realized, "Hell, I never even touched her!"

We made our way up the coast to San Diego, California. A bunch of us were taken on a little boat to our assigned ships. We saw all these destroyers and light cruisers and everything else. We finally got to the ship to which I'd been assigned. My God, it was huge. Destroyers were, and are, beautiful ships. They don't call them the "greyhounds of the sea" for nothing. Mine was an old four-stacker, which meant she was from World War I. She was actually built in 1917, the same year that I was born, and her name was the USS *Lamberton*.

I was told to take my stuff down below and get rid of the hammock. Here, you got a mattress and bunk. We were three deep, bunk style, but the beds hung from chains: one high, one middle and one on the bottom. I got there first and took the bottom. Easier to get in and out.

Most of the time we were towing targets for the fleet. By targets, I mean *huge* bull's-eyes that they could shoot at with their big guns. Sometimes the targets would overturn and we'd have to go out with a whaleboat and try to turn them back over again. That was risky work, since it was easy to slip overboard. We also had to take care never to go behind the target once it was set up, for obvious reasons.

That's no joke. Accidents happen. One day we were towing a target for these big aircraft carriers and suddenly we heard a whistle we weren't accustomed to. There was an airplane above us. A spotter, we called them. Instead of giving directions to hit the target, he had targeted the ship! The chief radioman darted for the radio and shouted for the ships to cease fire. What the hell. The military actually has a pretty good safety record, when you consider how many orders are going to so many people, most of whom are armed.

Apart from being shot at, the only thing that we grumbled about were the long boots we had to wear. If you got caught in the water with long boots on they'd fill up and take you down like a stone. We often made holes in the soles, just in case.

Hauling targets wasn't our only job, of course. We'd polish brass or scrub the sides of the ship to get rid of the rust or we'd paint the sides of the ship to cover the rust we couldn't scrape away. I was particularly interested in knowing what made this ship go, and took the wheel whenever I could. Today, they steer with a tiny lever that they just push or pull. But on my ship we had a great big wheel. You stood there for a two-hour shift, trying to keep it on course. Believe me, if that ship was working against a storm or any kind of waves you had to compensate all the time. It was really hard work. But there were times when the sea was calm and you'd steam right along and it was perfect. I was pretty good at manning the wheel and they put me on it when we were coming through the Panama Canal, both ways. Those were two of the greatest trips of my life!

But by far the biggest job most of us had was swabbing the deck. You need to keep it clean because you don't want people slipping on oil or little puddles of seawater—or vomit. Losing your lunch was a way of life. Our vessel only had a beam of about nineteen or twenty feet, which meant that when it hit a wave you got bounced around from side to side and up and down pretty good. It wasn't even a sign of weakness to throw up. The destroyer had a way of surprising you with new moves, and even seasoned sailors would lose their lunch.

A lot of the guys got sick right off the bat. We had one poor ensign who used to grab a box of crackers and sit over the hatch of the engine room to keep steady and warm. The captain would come by and just shake his head. There was never any question about whether he was faking it. The guy's skin color was lime green.

Me, I didn't get sick at all. Ever since that experience on the *Dante Alighieri*, my body seemed to understand that it had to adjust to being at sea. Maybe it's something you have to experience young, like getting a vaccination. The only thing that I did have to worry about were the bruises I got when I would hit the "knee knockers," the edge of the hatches leading to the living quarters. Sometimes the sea would swell and the old girl would pitch, or you'd come around the hatch too fast and *pow*, you'd hit one. You wanted to stop and punch something to help you forget the pain, but you had to keep going because there were people behind you. I've still got marks on my legs from where I whapped the hard metal.

Because of the long hours of hard labor, when we needed a break we'd go to the john. Our toilet consisted of a room that had water running through a trough along the side. One half of the trough was for urinals, the other had partitions where you would sit in small booths over the trough.

At any given time there'd be a bunch of guys sitting there, some actually using the john and some just reading a comic book. We had a bosun's mate named Claude Andrew Babcock. When his cigar was pointing down from his mouth, everything was fine. When it was standing up straight, watch out.

One day he comes into the john, without notice. We had no way of knowing his cigar was up . . . way up. He stood on the long side, set fire to a large wad of toilet paper, and when the water came sweeping through the trough to clean away the waste, he dropped the pile of burning paper. That fire hit us in the ass and, boy, we came bouncing out of there fast.

He said, "Now, get the hell back to work."

You talk about people moving in a hurry. Some of us who were there for legitimate reasons didn't even take time to wipe ourselves.

Most of the time, though, Babcock was a good guy. Unfortunately, things didn't end well for him. One day after I had been on board the ship a few days, I asked about the bunk next to mine. For some reason, no one had touched it. I asked one of the veteran sailors whose it was.

"Oh, you'll find out," he said.

Well, one morning I woke up and the bunk was occupied. I said, "Oh, my God."

The man who was lying in it had an erection so huge it actually lifted the blankets off his body.

Overall, it was a wonderful ship with the kind of camaraderie I've always enjoyed. The men would work together, take shore leave together, shop for the folks back home together, eat Chinese food and visit whorehouses together, usually in that order.

I felt good about my life and experiences, but in one respect I wasn't getting anywhere. In those days ranks were practically frozen. They had all the higher ranking men they could possibly handle. I made seaman second class, and took the test for seaman first. I passed that. So I was making a fat $63.00 a month, $2.00 a day. That's not to be sneezed at. But I had ambition and I wanted to get off the deck force, if I possibly could.

One day the new bosun's mate—who was aware of my dissatisfaction—came over to me and said, "We've got an opening in the galley. You want to be a cook?"

I said, "Hell, yes," so I went to the galley and learned new skills. I cooked everything on the menu—except for spaghetti. I could have made the greatest spaghetti for them, but, I swear, I never landed that assignment. I always got fried oysters or baked beans or hamburgers or potatoes, mashed or hashed or French fried. I even learned to make my own corn bread. But never pasta. Go figure.

Cooking was fun for me, but it was hard in one way. The galley would make you perspire, so much so that you'd have to step outside with just a T-shirt to get a little fresh air. Now, it can get pretty cold and windy on deck, and I started to cough.

Pretty soon they noticed that I was really hacking.

I was sent to see the doc, who told me I had bronchitis. Rather than have me cough all over the food, they put me back on deck—though they gave me relatively easy details since I wasn't in great shape. Then one day an officer came over and said, "Hey we've got an opening for you. How'd you like to become a gunner's mate?"

I said, "That'll suit me fine." So I started studying all about the guns on the ship—firing, cleaning, painting, assembling, and disassembling. I even studied the blueprints. I became a third-class gunner's mate, then a second-class gunner's mate, and finally a first-class gunner's mate. By that time I'd been aboard for four years and I reenlisted for two more.

No sooner had I learned a new set of skills than somebody up top got an idea that we should become a high-speed minesweeper. That meant charging ahead with this mine apparatus that we had, a big paravane that went down into the water and stretched before us. If it ran up against any mine without the ship hitting it first, you were in good shape. If not, you were sunk. Literally. Upon snagging a mine, a sharp wire would cut the chain automatically and bring the explosive to the surface. There, we were supposed to detonate it by shooting it.

Well, we never did see a mine. I later learned that during World War II the *Lamberton* ran up against a lot of mines around Alaska. I sort of wish I'd been there for that. You form a bond with your ship. You really do. If she's in danger, you want to be there looking out for her.

Aside from nearly getting blown up by one of our own aircraft, the second worst day of my military career came when I was put in charge of the captain's gig, a long, light boat reserved for his use. I was the skipper. That was the epitome, let me tell you, to be chauffeuring the top brass to shore. I polished that sucker until it shined. I couldn't wait for the skipper to come down for the first time so I could take him ashore.

They finally called for the gig to take the skipper ashore. I was dressed to the nines. I had my hat on perfect and I brought the gig alongside. The engineer clicked the bell to signal that we were in position. The skipper came down the gangway and he looked at me and said, "128th Street, New York City."

I said, "Yes, sir."

Well, I had polished that boat so beautifully that as I pushed away from the gangplank my foot slipped. I went into the drink between the gangway and the boat with a huge splash.

I came back up again, sputtering under my hat. The captain looked down at me and he said, "No, no, son. I said, '128th Street.'"

I'm sure he must have been laughing, because the engineer sure was, I'll tell you, I scurried back to where I belonged and then steered away. But I'll never forget that day as long as I live. Neither did he. When he left the ship for good, I took him ashore and he turned and said to me, "I'll never forget you, Borgnine, checking the bottom of the boat for me."

I said, "Thank you, sir. Thank you for remembering."

He was a good skipper, too.

The *Lamberton* was a radio-controlled vessel. That meant in case of war, they could sail her without a crew. The plan was to fill it with explosives and explode it in some port they wanted to disable. There were two RCVs: the *Lamberton* and the *Boggs*. Years later, in Hollywood, the famous show business columnist Army Archerd came up to me and said, "You were in the navy?"

I said "Yes, sir. I was onboard a ship called the USS *Lamberton*."

He looked rather strangely at me and said, "Did you ever hear of the USS *Boggs*?"

I said, "Sure. That was the ship right next to us in the nest."

He said, "I was aboard the *Boggs*."

It is indeed a small world.

In our newest configuration as an RCV, we were sent to Honolulu. However, before leaving San Diego I did manage to get my heart broken a little.

I had this buddy, Vincent Lang. We went ashore and met a couple of girls, a rather tall one and a one a little bit shorter but still taller than either of us. We got to talking to them and started seeing them every time we went ashore. One day we got a car and took the girls up to see the stars at the San Diego planetarium. We had a wonderful day and became kind of chummy and one thing led to another.

No, not that. I mean, we fell in love.

Her name was Millie and I met her father, who thought I was quite a guy. When I shipped out to Hawaii, we promised to stay in touch and I said I'd hop a ship back to the States whenever I could. But one incredibly hot day in Honolulu I got a Dear John letter saying, "I'm sorry, but now I'm married very happily, thank you very much."

The temperature dropped about twenty degrees for me.

I was heartbroken, but what are you going to do? We actually did stay in touch, and some years later I was doing the play *Harvey* on the road with my then-wife Rhoda. We were booked into Minneapolis-St. Paul, where Millie lived. I invited her and Vincent Lang's wife—because he'd been lucky enough to marry his girl—to come see the show.

I remember Rhoda and Millie talking and looking at me and occasionally laughing. I guessed they were bonding over the crazy guy one had ducked and one hadn't. We're good friends to this day, which is more than I can say for most of the women I loved and married.

Upon reaching Honolulu we tied up in Pearl City. They put us in the backwaters of Honolulu Harbor and there we stayed. We discovered this was not a good place for us. If the wind was just right, our ships would be black in the morning from the residue when the sugarcane fields were burned. That was a process which started many years before, when one sugarcane farmer took a dislike to another and set fire to the other guy's sugarcane fields. But the plan backfired when the victim discovered that the fire burned off all the leaves, saving the harvesters extra work. From then on they all burned their fields.

When the ships were black with soot, guess who had to clean them up?

If you ever wanted to hear unvarnished naval swearing—and I can't imagine why you would—that was the place for it. The burnt sugar mixed with the salty air and formed a hard substance that clung to the hull like plastic. I used to think, "Where are those misguided spotter planes when you need 'em to blast something?"

Apart from that, Hawaii was great. The climate wasn't as chilly and misty as San Diego. We all knew our jobs so well by this time that work didn't always feel like work, and leave was like a real vacation. We would go ashore and catch a bus going into downtown Honolulu. They paid us all on different paydays—the army was one week, the navy another—so that never the twain should meet. Because if we all went drinking on the same night, there would always be a fight over a slur or a girl or somebody's home state.

There was an ambitious young gentleman, a Japanese guy, who started selling beer on the corner where you caught the bus. First thing you know he was making so much money just selling beer to the sailors that he opened up a big place with a dance floor. We later came to find out that it was also a great place for spies. They could hear exactly where we were going, what we were doing. I'm sure they had spies all over the place telling them what to hit when they fired on Hawaii.

When we were on ship, the commanders started a routine of having our planes fly over for what they called a drill. Everybody went to their general quarters battle stations. Our guns would follow these airplanes. We did that for a half to three-quarters of an hour and then they'd go away. We'd secure everything and go back about our business. That was done six days a week. Things were dicey in Europe— this was 1940—but we didn't really think we were at risk in Hawaii. And if anything did happen, we felt we were prepared.

But the Japanese were a little smarter. They came on a Sunday, December 7, 1941, when everybody was resting. The rest is history, of course.

I wasn't there when it all came down. I had finished up in September, 1941. The *Lamberton* also missed that initial action. When

Honolulu was attacked, my girl was out at sea pulling targets for the fleet. In fact, most of the firing ships, the aircraft carriers, had stayed at sea over the weekend to prepare for target practice Monday morning. But word reached me at home in Connecticut that the *Lamberton* actually saw those airplanes coming in toward Honolulu. They radioed in and said "There are a bunch of planes coming in with red balls on their wings."

The guys on the radar reported it and heard back, "Oh, yeah, that's fine. Those are our planes coming in from the States." But they weren't coming in from the States, they were coming in from Japanese ships to the west. It's easy to second-guess decisions with hindsight, but I wonder how many lives could have been saved if the boys on the other end of that call had bothered to look at a map.

The executive officer who was on board when I left the ship was kind of a nasty guy, and Italian to boot. He was real mad because I could speak Italian and he couldn't. I used to call him names, but he couldn't do anything about it because I said them nicely and he didn't know what they meant. When he knew I was leaving, he said to me, "What do you think you're doing? We're practically at war and you won't re-up?"

I said, "No, sir. I want to go home. My mom isn't well and I want to spend some time with her."

He looked at me and said, "Well, enjoy marching in the rear rank while we're marching up front holding Old Glory."

That hurt, because no one loved the United States more than I did. But I didn't answer. I didn't want to spend my last enlisted days in the brig. But that wasn't the last time I saw him. Years later, I was in Norfolk, Virginia, doing something with the Barter Theatre. I was in this paint shop buying paint for the show. I looked up and there was this old exec of mine.

I said, "Well, sir. How are you?"

He glanced over. "Oh," he said. "You're Borgnine."

I said, "That's right, sir. I'm the guy you said would be marching in the rear rank."

In fact, I hadn't been—not exactly—but we'll get to that in a moment.

He said, "Well, Borgnine, I had three ships shot out from under me. Can you match that?"

I told him I couldn't and said that I was glad he'd made it. Then I told him that I'd been acting and gave him tickets to the show.

He said, "Okay, I'll be there."

I never did see him again. Still, I don't think ill of him. I can't. Not of a man who served his country the way he did.

Chapter 8

Home Again ... but Not for Long

I left the *Lamberton* and was transferred home. They sent me to New London, Connecticut, which was about an hour from my house.

I hadn't been there for years. The last time I'd gone had been a sad occasion. Not long after I signed up, my ship was docked in Guantánamo Bay, Cuba. This was long before Castro. Cuba was full of friendly, generally happy folks who used to make good rice bread. It was miserably hot and humid there and most of us slept on deck. We'd bring our mattresses up from their swinging hooks and lay them down. You'd have to deal with the flies, but that was better than the heat belowdecks.

Anyway, I was on watch one night and somebody came to me and said, "Borgnine, we just got notice that your grandmother has passed away."

That's the military for you: unsentimental and to the point.

While I waited to see if I could get leave to go home, I started thinking about my father's mother. I'm sure you've experienced this: the passing of a loved one brings about all kinds of wistful thinking. The tears would come at some point, probably at her funeral. Then and there, on that dark deck, was a time for remembering.

My grandmother lived nearby and during the summer I would spend a few weeks at her house, helping with her garden and washing and sterilizing bottles for the root beer she made and sold. Like Mrs. Simone and her pizza, my grandmother could have gotten rich off her root beer.

I had a friend in that neighborhood, Spenny Holtz. One time my grandmother caught us smoking in the bathroom. Not cigarettes, which we couldn't afford, but corn silk that we saved after eating corn on the cob in some poor farmer's field. Well, this little old lady just tore down the house.

"Out!" she screamed, grabbing me by the hair and hauling me all the way home. I knew she wouldn't tell my mother, because she didn't want my mother to worry about anything, since her health was fragile. But she laid the law down. She said "From now on, you don't do that."

Not only didn't I smoke, but I would get a little tingle of fear every time I ate corn on the cob. My grandmother was strict!

I was given permission to go home for the funeral. When I got there, I found out that Joey had just joined the navy, too, and was waiting to ship out. We had lost touch and neither of us knew the other had enlisted. It was good seeing him again, more man than boy now. He introduced me to one of his neighbors, a woman named Victoria Warwick, who was a palm reader. She asked us to let her tell our fortunes. We didn't believe in any of that, but figured we had nothing to lose.

She took Joey's hand and said, "You're in the navy now, and that's wonderful. You'll be okay on the sea, but something will ail you. I don't know what it is, but you should be careful."

Then she looked at my hand and she was thunderstruck. She said, "You're never gonna have to work hard in all your life. You're going to be very rich and you'll do something that's extremely different."

That made absolutely no sense at all, but I thanked her and we left.

As it all turned out, Joey came home from the navy shortly before

I did, suffering from ulcers. I heard he wasn't well and as soon as I arrived I went to see him. I have since changed my mind about Mrs. Warwick, wherever she is. Sadly, the fortune-teller had nailed it.

Joey was very sick due to internal bleeding and died not long after. I was able to visit him just one more time at his home and he didn't look well. I knew the end was near. I wanted to see him again after that, but I didn't get the chance. Maybe it's just as well, because I remember him now as the scrappy little kid who used to filch celery with me.

God bless him.

No sooner had I gotten home than we got a telephone call from a neighbor who asked if we were listening to the radio. We weren't, and he said, "Turn it on, quick!"

We heard that Pearl Harbor had been bombed. I thought of my crewmates, my ship, my country. I remember thinking, "Oh, my God, what am I going to do?"

I went and got out my uniform and my mother said, "No, no, please. Don't go. Wait till they call you."

I said, "Mom, I've got to go!"

She said, "No! I want you to wait until they call you."

Well, she probably saved my life. Had I gone then, I'd have been one of the first men sent to the South Pacific, where our early losses were horrendous. So I went to work at a construction site and one day she called the office and asked to speak with me. She said, in a strong voice that gave me courage, "You got a card. You have to go."

I went home and put on my first-class gunner's mate uniform. I went to the local recruiting station and was told to report to the First Naval District in New York City. When I arrived, they looked up my name and said, "Oh, yes. You've got in-shore patrol over here at 125th Street."

Okay—I knew what shore patrol was, but I had no idea what *in-*

shore patrol might be. Walking the docks? Checking for mines or enemy submarines?

No.

He said, "They've got a boat up at 125th Street that picks up the kids from Columbia University to teach them the rudiments of guns and everything. That's where they want you."

They signed me up and I went aboard ship. It was a converted yacht called the *Sylph*, donated to the Navy to help in the war against subs on the Atlantic. It belonged to the man who invented the Murphy bed.

I spent my first night aboard the *Sylph* in a comfortable bunk in my own cabin. The next morning this guy by the name of Borguignon came to introduce me to the skipper. Everybody called him "Borgi 1" and me "Borgi 2." We went up and knocked on the skipper's door. We heard a "Yes, who's there?"

I said, "Borgnine, sir, a new first-class gunner's mate who's just come aboard."

He said, "Just a moment."

We heard some fiddling around with the door and finally he said "Okay, come in." We walked in and the skipper was still in his bunk. He had a hand underneath his pillow and was looking up. It was like we'd caught him with a girlie magazine or something. I gave him my credentials and told him where I came from and what I had been doing.

He said, "Okay, have Borguignon show you around."

As we started to leave he got up on one elbow. I saw his pillow flip over and there was a .45 in his hand. We got the hell out of there in a hurry. I later found out the captain was frightened of a certain character aboard ship, the chief carpenter's mate. The guy hated the assignment because he stood around doing nothing most of the time, and he didn't like the skipper, who was always on his tail yelling at him to find something *to* do. Well, there just wasn't a lot of repair work or maintenance, so the carpenter got a lot of shore leave. Then he'd come aboard drunk and would yell down through the ventilator, "You son-of-a-bitch dirty bastard! Come up here, I'll kill you, you no-good bastard."

I asked Borgi 1 why the skipper took that. He said the skinny little guy was just afraid of the big carpenter. Period.

The chief carpenter's mate kept putting in for a transfer and one day Washington granted his request. So they transferred him to a great big vessel that was going to take stuff over to England, carrying planes and everything. He left happy, knowing he'd be setting sail in less than a week.

About three days later, the captain himself got orders to leave and guess where he went? To the same ship where the carpenter's mate had gone! Well, he had no intention of going and that ship sailed without him. It was the last time the ship was ever seen. It got caught in a hundred-mile-an-hour gale off Newfoundland and went down. But that's not the end of the story. The carpenter was the only one who was not lost at sea. He said he refused to drown because he hated the captain so much and wouldn't give him the satisfaction.

I lost track of both men after that, though if the carpenter's still around I'm sure his hate is as rich and deep as it was sixty-seven years ago!

After that skipper left we had another guy who was a lieutenant junior grade and they gave him command of the USS *Sylph*. He was a Yale graduate and still pretty much of a frat boy. He got along great with the kids from Columbia.

Throughout the war I found myself hopscotching up and down the East Coast from Rhode Island to Florida on a variety of assignments. One day I was sitting on the john—in my private john, naturally—and there was a knock on the door.

The seaman said, "Guess what?"

"What?" I asked, annoyed. Couldn't this wait?

"They just dropped a bomb on Japan that was the equivalent to about twenty tons of TNT. It wiped out everything as far as the eye could see."

I said to myself "What a stupid thing? How can one bomb possibly do all that?"

Well, we turned on the radio and there it was. The United States had dropped the first atomic bomb on Japan, on the city of Hiroshima. The writing was on the wall. We were all quite exuberant about it.

Three days later President Truman gave the order to drop a second bomb, this time on Nagasaki.

Those two bombs undoubtedly saved the lives of millions on both sides. The Japanese were not afraid. I mean, they were still fighting valiantly and we had barely scratched their homeland. And now it was over. No more of our boys, or theirs, no more mothers' sons, had to die. That's why I consider to this day that President Truman was one of the most wonderful presidents we've had since Lincoln.

Delighted as I was, I now had to face something I hadn't had to deal with for nearly ten years:

"Okay, kid. You're twenty-eight. What do you do with the rest of your life?"

Chapter 9

Postwar Blues

Now that the war was over and I was out of the navy, I went home again. I still didn't know what to do. Once again, my mother made up my mind for me—sort of.

She said, "Well? Are you going to get a job or not?"

That may sound like an option, but it wasn't.

So I went out looking for work. Not a job, not a career—just any kind of labor. That was pretty much all that was available, due to the slowdown of the war industries. Plus a lot of men—and women—had grabbed the available jobs in my absence. I'd pack a lunch and stand in front of one of the local factories and watch the folks walking into shops. After just a few days of this, with nothing to show but goose-bumps from an early fall, I decided this wasn't what I wanted to do. Not after everything I'd seen and learned and experienced in the navy. After being on the sea or in big, open ports, going into a factory would be like going to jail.

Instead, I'd take my lunch and I'd go to a park or go to a movie. It was like *The Full Monty*, but without the nudity.

One day I came home and I guess I looked despondent. My mother asked me what was the matter.

I said, "Mom, for two cents I'd go back and join the navy again. At least I'd get a pension at the end of my twenty years."

I wasn't sure whether she'd approve or disapprove. All I know is I didn't expect what she actually said to me.

"Son," she said, "have you ever thought of becoming an actor?"

If I was, my reaction didn't show it. Instead of being cool and thoughtful, I was openly, over-the-top flabbergasted. I made a few inarticulate sounds—"What? Huh?" that sort of thing—as she went on.

"You always like to make a damn fool of yourself, making people laugh. Why don't you give it a try?"

I looked at her, still not sure what to say, and so help me I saw these doors open and a light shined down from the heavens. That smart, worldly, perceptive woman was right, even if she maybe could have couched it a little nicer. But then, that was my mother.

I said, "Mom, that's what I'm going to be."

Now that the Big Question had been decided, I had no idea where to go, what to do, who to see. Show business? What's show business? We had a radio—TV was still three years off—and we'd listen to the fights or Jack Benny or Eddie Cantor. We knew that much about show business, but that was it.

Well, before it faded, that same golden light gave me an idea. Yale University was in New Haven, which was right next door. They had a world-famous drama department. I'd go there for advice.

The next day I hitchhiked over to see if I could get into the Yale School of Drama on the G.I. Bill. For those of you who don't know, the G.I. Bill of Rights was passed in 1944 to finance the training and education of soldiers who had been out of the civilian job market during the war. It was a lifesaver for many veterans who, like myself, had skills that couldn't be applied to nonmilitary occupations. There just wasn't a lot of call for kids who could operate a 102-mm gun.

I went to see a Professor Cole, who was the head of the school. He looked at my marks from high school—and my decade-long service record—and said, "Yes, we'll be able to admit you. But it will first re-quire two years of undergraduate study."

I said, "What will those studies consist of, sir?" thinking they'd be things like costume design and lighting and maybe photography.

He said, "Trigonometry, calculus, physics, chemistry."

Good thing I was sitting. I felt my legs get wobbly, like the first time I'd set foot on the *Lamberton*. He had named everything that I hated in high school. The only reason they passed me was because I was a good kid.

I said, "Sir, I don't mean to be disrespectful, but I don't want to be a mathematician or a scientist. I want to be an actor."

He said, "The university requires everyone to have a full and rounded education."

I thanked him very much and left, dejected. Ever notice how learning something usually doesn't give you the result you hoped for?

But I wasn't about to give up. Asking around at other schools—those with a little less ivy—I finally found out about the Randall School up in Hartford, Connecticut. I took a bus from New Haven. They were glad to see me. They didn't care what credentials I had. Thanks to my enthusiasm and the government funding, the head of the school interviewed me, then said, "I'll sign you up right now."

Because the semester had just started, I went to my first class right then and there. I was giddy with terror and excitement as he took me to the front of the class and introduced me. I felt like I was among kindred souls, yet not. I was twenty-eight years old and had just completed ten years in the navy. Everyone else was eighteen, or nineteen, and had just graduated from high school. Judging from their big eyes and fresh faces, most had never left the city, let alone the state. I later learned that some were here because they loved acting, some because they were lousy students at everything else, and some because they wanted to meet spouses.

For that day's class they were all reading Thomas Wolfe's *You Can't Go Home Again*. The teacher handed me a copy, showed me to an empty seat, and after they'd read for a while, the teacher said, "Mr. Borgnine, would you mind reading the next few paragraphs?" Talk about stage fright! I'd never read in front of people before.

I started to read and I was doing pretty well. There was a description of America at night. I read, "And the stars were shining like diamonds."

She stopped me and said, "Mr. Borgnine, how do you pronounce the word d-i-a-m-o-n-d-s?"

I looked at her, then at the book, and I said "Dimonds."

She said, "No. The word is Di-a-monds."

I looked at the word for a moment and said, "Oh, shit," out loud.

It brought down the house. I'll bet it was the first time some of those kids actually heard the word. You get some kind of education in the navy, let me tell you.

Cool as a radio operator, the teacher said, "No, the word is still 'diamonds.'"

Everybody laughed harder.

It wasn't a very orthodox introduction to the world of acting, but I knew at the time that was a good thing. I liked the challenge, having to regain my balance, and making people react to something I'd done.

Four months later I had the lead in an important play by Norman Corwin about VE Day. I got the first rave reviews given to an actor at this school in fourteen years. I was proud, but I was also restless. Despite the fun and the acclaim, I decided I didn't want to be an actor. It was hurry up and wait. Wait for someone else's scene to be rehearsed. Wait for the lights to be set. Wait for the scenery to be finished. Wait for the audience to find their seats. I'd had enough waiting in the navy. So I told the dean I was leaving. Much to my surprise the ordinarily sweet and supportive head of the school hit me on the hand with a ruler.

"How can you leave?" he said. "You have a God-given gift for the theater."

"But I'm bored a lot of the time," I replied. "I need to be doing things."

Looking back, I can understand why Professor Cole had insisted I improve my mind at Yale. But back then, I only knew I was restless. I had that much of my father in me: he was a restless doer, too.

"I'll tell you what," he said. "Instead of rushing to get home each day, take a later bus. Talk to some of the kids. See what they're thinking, what they want to do."

It proved to be good advice.

One of the kids I knew a little at the Randall School was Fred Dimek. When I told him how I was feeling, he said to me, "I feel the same."

I said, "Huh?"

"Yeah," he went on. "I want to get out there in the real world, where you've been. I want to see if I've got what it takes."

He told me he'd been accepted as part of the repertory company by an organization called the Barter Theatre of Virginia.

"Why don't you come down with me?" he suggested. "Stay a couple of days, see what it's all about. If it's any good, then, hey, who knows? Maybe they'll take you, too."

What he was really saying was, "*If you're any good . . .*" But I didn't mind. He was right. If I were any good, maybe they'd take me, too.

I said okay and, two days later we were on the overnight train to Abingdon, Virginia.

Chapter 10

All the World Really Is a Stage

We got off that old rattler feeling dirty, disheveled, and exhausted. There were numerous delays due to track problems and I felt like my butt had been permanently flattened from having sat in that thinly cushioned seat. In the cool early morning, we walked up a hill toward the Barter Inn, where my buddy had been told to go. We waited there for Mr. Robert Porterfield, the head of the theater.

Mr. Porterfield arrived late in the morning, looked at Fred, and said, "Well, you didn't show up on time, so we filled your position."

We were both too tired to react. When the words sunk in, I wanted to pop the guy.

But then he said, "If you want to work on costumes or something like that, you're welcome to stay."

To my surprise, Fred said, "No, no, thank you."

I guess he never heard of the concept of getting your foot in the door.

Mr. Porterfield looked at me. "And what do you do?"

I said, "Well, ah—I'm an actor."

"I'm up to here in actors," he said, indicating the chin where I'd been thinking of hitting him. "But if you're willing to work in the scene docks and things like that, we'll put you to work. I'll give you three squares a day and a place to sleep."

That sounded okay to me—the navy without the water. I replied, "Well, that sounds pretty good."

Fred went back to Hartford, dejected, and I found myself working in the scenery docks. I was put in the charge of an actor named George Burns—he later changed his name to Bart Burns because they already had a George Burns in show business. Burns had "Captain, U.S. Marine Corps" sewn on the sleeve of his jacket. When we were introduced, I said, "How're you doing, sir?"

"Fine," he said curtly—intrigued that I'd called him "sir" but suspicious, because marines tend to give the time of day only to marines.

"So, what the hell are we supposed to be doing here?"

"We're washing the paint off these old flats so they can be used in new sets," he said.

"Just like I used to on my destroyer," I replied.

So now he knew I wasn't USMC. I waited to see how he would react.

He just looked at me and grinned. "Welcome to showbiz, Borgnine."

We became good friends.

I worked my fool head off. At night, after I had my dinner at the Barter Inn, I used to go over to the theater and watch them work. I'd sit in the balcony and I'd be a critic. I liked what this one did, I liked what that one did, maybe not so much with this one, and so on. I thought about how I would have played it, memorizing some of the lines and running the scene in my head. God, it felt good. The navy had become my home, but sitting up here the theater immediately felt like a new home. And no disrespect to Yale University or the Randall School, but *this* was how you trained and educated an aspiring actor. The old-fashioned way, by having him apprentice in a real-life setting to learn the trade. That's something we've lost in our overeducated modern world.

Finally, after I'd been there a few months, Mr. Porterfield said to me, "Didn't you tell me you were an actor?"

I blurted, "Yes! Yes!"

He said, "Well, now's your chance to prove it."

They needed somebody to play a union leader in *State of the Union*.

"I accept!" I said. "Where are my sides?" (For all you nonactors, those are the pages of script that have your lines, your part on them.)

"There are no sides," Mr. Porterfield told me. "All you do is cross from one side of the stage to the other and just look important as hell."

I was a little disappointed, but I absolutely refused to show it. That's acting, too. I said okay: it was a part.

I went to wardrobe and got myself a coat with a vest. I got a cigar and when they told me to walk I put the cigar in my mouth and I walked across the stage with my finger in my vest. Let me tell you something: I never felt as alive as I did when I walked from the wings and those bright lights hit me. Despite what they show you in the movies, you can't see more than a row or two into a theater. But you can sure feel everyone out there. You can feel them watching you, and that magnifies every nerve in your body, every sense you have. You feel alive at a level that renews itself from second to second. It just doesn't get better than that.

Naturally, there was a local critic in the audience on opening night. Her review was lukewarm, but she said that of all the people in that show, the only one who made an impression on her was me.

"Here was a man who literally stole the show. All he did was walk across the stage, but he captivated you."

Of course, my brain told me that not every review I'd ever get would be that good, but I didn't care. Right then it was the shot I needed. I sent it to my mom and she wrote back that she couldn't be prouder. That meant even more to me than the review.

Unfortunately, mom didn't get to read too many more of those.

Mom passed away a few weeks later. I was toggling between acting and working on the sets. We had just finished a show and were packing up when Larry Gates, one of the actors in the show, came up to me and said, "Ernie, I've got some bad news for you."

I said, "What is it?"

He said, "There was a call during the show. Your mom just passed away."

I started to cry as I helped pack away all the stuff. Everyone gave me space. I tried to think of what my mother would want me to do. I had obligations here and I said that to the cast. But everyone said, "No, no, you've got to go home."

They were right. I made arrangements to leave the next day. I sat outside on the loading dock and cried all night long, out loud. I cried myself out.

The next morning I caught the train to go home. I couldn't cry any more. I was just thinking of all the things that had happened in my lifetime with my mother. I said to myself "I've lost my life. I've lost the person that I love the most alongside my dad." My dad lived long enough to see me become a star. But my mother was the one who gave me the inspiration and she barely got to see any of it.

It wasn't fair. But it wasn't fair about Joey dying, either. Or Pearl Harbor being attacked. "Fair" just isn't on life's menu.

When I got home I felt better. I saw Mom in her coffin, and the last thing that my sister and I did was something my mother had actually discussed with her. My mother loved whipped cream. We used to take a little bottle of heavy cream and we'd whip it up for her. She would just adore it.

One day she had said, "When I pass away some day maybe you could put a bottle of whipped cream in my coffin so I'll have it when I get up to St. Peter's gate."

Evie and I were both standing by the open coffin and I looked at her and she looked at me and I didn't have to say a word. My little smile said it all.

"No," she insisted. "We shouldn't do that."

I said, "Why not? You know she'll be happy."

But my sister insisted it was disrespectful and I yielded to her wishes. To this day I kick myself in the behind for not having done it.

I stayed in Connecticut for a week. After making sure that my sis and Dad were okay, I returned to Virginia ready to honor my mother's faith in me. During that next year I acted more and painted less. I was in fourteen different shows. Then, thanks to a rave review that somehow made its way to an agent's desk in New York, I got the call to go to Broadway. Brock Pemberton, the theatrical producer, had seen me in Virginia and offered me the part of Wilson, the attendant in the mental hospital in Mary Chase's hit comedy *Harvey*. I would be replacing Jesse White (the original Maytag repairman on those commercials), who was leaving.

I finished in Virginia and flew that night to New York. I figured Broadway was worth the extravagance. Plus, there wasn't time to take the train.

I reported to the theater as instructed. Mind you, this was opening day for previews. The director was busy, so the stage manager took me to his small office, walked me through the play, a comedy, and after a few scenes said, "You'll do."

That wasn't a rousing commendation, but it was enough to get me the gig. I didn't believe it would always be so easy. But they were up against an opening date, I'd gotten good notices in a similar part, it was a small role, and the tumblers had just fallen into place.

The stage manager gave me the script and told me to learn the lines. Boy, did I cram. All those nights sitting in the balcony of the Barter, memorizing what the actors said onstage, had paid off. The first time I met the cast was when I walked onstage in front of the audience.

You know that *super-reality* I mentioned that comes from being onstage? Not this time. The whole thing was a blur. I was nervous and perspiring and living from moment to moment as I tried to keep the lines in my head and respond to what the other actors were giving me. In other words, to act.

After the show, still in a daze, I got myself a hotel room—I didn't know where else to stay—and walked up to a place at the end of 48th Street and Broadway. I hadn't eaten and I was starving. As I sat at the counter, I was finally starting to relax.

I thought, *"Goddamn, Borgnine, you did it! You've conquered the Great White Way!"* It seemed like yesterday that I was here on inshore duty for the navy and didn't know what I wanted to do with my life. Now I was a Broadway actor. It was amazing.

I was in another world, but I came back to this one fast. Some woman walked by who had just seen the show and she said, "There's that jerk who was talking between the laughs. What a bore!" (She obviously had no idea that's how the play was written, but that didn't make me feel any better.)

Well, it burst my bubble. So much for being a conqueror.

The director gave me a few notes and that night I really tried to get in there and do it right. I did better, of course, and the reviewers were eventually pretty kind. After about a month, though, I realized I wasn't happy. Something just wasn't clicking and I knew what it was: I didn't have enough experience, yet, for the big time. I'm not being unduly modest; it just takes more confidence than I had at the time. I went back to Brock Pemberton—our producer, and one of the founders of Broadway's famed Tony Awards—and said "Sir, I've got to leave."

"What d'ya mean you got to leave?" he said. "Where you going?"

"Back to the Barter Theatre."

"Leave Broadway for regional? What the hell for?"

I was too embarrassed to tell him the real reason, so I gave him another—which was also true. "Well, you know, Mr. Porterfield gave me my first break and did so much for me and I feel I owe him a debt of gratitude."

Mr. Pemberton said, "Gratitude, my ass! He never paid you anything. I'm giving you $150 a week and you feel you got to go back there for gratitude?"

"Yes, sir."

He grinned. "Well, okay. Good luck and I hope we'll see you again."

He was a wonderful guy. I don't know what actor got my part, but I hope it did better for him than it did for me!

I went back to Virginia with a vengeance, determined to learn my craft. As it happened, no sooner had I returned than I was put into *Hamlet*, of all things—the ultimate theatrical man killer. Fortunately, I wasn't playing the Dane.

I didn't let Shakespeare faze me, not even when I heard that the State Department was interested in sponsoring the troupe on an overseas engagement. They wanted us to perform *Hamlet* at Kronberg Castle in Elsinore, Denmark—where the play supposedly had its historical roots.

A deal was worked out where Uncle Sam would cover our expenses and handle all the publicity. Okay, I guess you could call it propaganda: Washington wanted to help repopulate the war-weary world with culture as well as food and industry.

The reviews weren't the most glowing in the history of theater. Seems the Danes didn't like Brits playing Danes, and they appreciated Americans even less. But what the heck. I sure didn't come out of the experience empty-handed. I got to channel historical people—figuratively, of course—and it was a valuable acting lesson about opening myself up to the environment. I also got to see some of Europe. The Air Force took us around to all these different places. I got to see Hitler's Eagle's Nest. We also saw Dachau, where this sergeant reached into an oven and pulled out something charred. I looked at it and said, "What is it?" Mind you, there had been some stories written about the concentration camps, but not a lot.

He said, "A human bone. They burned people in here." He handed it to me. "Take this back and show it to the people at home. This will prove what these bastards were doing."

I didn't take it, of course, but gently replaced the bone in the oven. I was assured the remains were going to be interred with respect.

When we walked through the yard there, it seemed like the sun became clouded over. Maybe it did, or maybe it just felt that way. It was a terrible experience. It reminded me of one of the reasons we had fought this war, why it was sometimes necessary to go to such lengths to remove despots and genocidal maniacs.

I learned a lot during our monthlong run in Denmark, and then back in Virginia. I gained the confidence I felt I had lacked the first time I was on Broadway. At the end of that season, I said, "Mr. Porter-field, I'm going back to New York."

He said, "I'm not surprised. You're a talented kid, Ernie. Do you have any idea what you're going to do?"

I said, "I'm going to try to get into theater and into this new thing they've got up there, television."

He said, "Good luck." I knew he meant it.

And I knew something else: I'd need it.

Chapter 11

Escape to New York

When I hit Penn Station, I wasn't alone. I had a wife.

Her name was Rhoda Kemins and she was a Navy Wave and a hospital corpswoman. She made an impression on me in 1945 when I was in the naval hospital with a cyst on my backside. And I made an impression on her. She figured she'd seen the worst part of me already and everything else would be uphill. We had a date when I got out of the hospital and then a few more until I went home. My mother hadn't met her, but she heard the way I talked about her and was convinced that we'd end up together.

I said, "No, Ma. She won't marry me. She's Jewish and she can only marry a Jewish man."

My mother just shook her head and said, "You keep her in mind."

I did. Her family lived in Brooklyn. When the war was over she moved back with them and started writing to me.

My mother read her letters. She said, "You should propose to her. She's going to make a good wife for you."

I went to New York to see her, and we carried on a long-distance romance for four years. Finally, when I decided to try my luck on Broadway, we tied the knot.

We stayed for a while with her folks and then we moved to our own place in Queens. It was a thirty-minute subway ride to Times Square and it was all we could afford.

I was thirty-three years old and, in many ways, I was starting from scratch. An agent got me in to see a few casting directors, but mostly I went to open calls, things you'd read about in *Back Stage* and other trade papers. These are the infamous "cattle calls" where you and every other actor in town would sign in, then stand around in a theater or loft waiting to be seen. The typical wait time was two or three hours. The length of the typical audition was one minute or under. The shortest audition I ever had was about ten seconds: I walked in and they didn't even hand me the script. The director just looked me up and down and said, "Next!"

Meanwhile, I had to earn money, so I took any work I could get. Washing dishes, unloading trucks, working in baggage rooms at the train terminals.

I began to miss the Barter Theatre, where you always knew what you'd be doing next. You had a little part in this one, or a little part in that one. You were always working and learning. Then suddenly, you're in a world where you're constantly being told, "No, nothing today."

Fortunately, theater wasn't the only place where a New York actor could find work in those days. There was a new kid in town, television. Not a lot of "legitimate" actors wanted to play there because it was rushed, crude, and only a handful of people even had TV sets. But I wasn't picky, and when I went to audition for a director, Robert Mulligan—he later went on to direct the movies *To Kill a Mockingbird* and *Summer of '42*—at NBC, I caught a break. He looked at me and said "Here, take this script. Take it home and read it. Come back tomorrow morning ."

I said, "Sir, I'd like to read it for you right now."

He said, "I'm busy."

I don't know what possessed me to say, "Me, too," but, luckily, he didn't take offense. He grinned and said, "Take five minutes, go out here on the fire escape, read this thing, then come back." So I went out for five minutes, read, and came back and we went through it.

When we finished he looked at me and he threw the script on the floor. "Goddamn it!"

I said, "Did I do something wrong?"

"No. You just gave me a whole new way to do this show."

Well, I ended up teaching Mark Twain how to pilot a boat up the Mississippi on the *Goodyear Television Playhouse*. That was my first show on television. I tried hard and they were very happy with me.

One thing led to another. Mulligan introduced me to Delbert Mann, one of the hot young directors in this new medium. Delbert took me under his wing. Every time you worked with Delbert it was like learning a whole new way of acting. He was resourceful, unpredictable, creative, and articulate. I've been fortunate to have a number of mentors in my life, but Delbert was without a doubt the most important.

As much as this was a time of personal growth and change, it was also a time of change in the country. We'd gone from a hot war to a Cold War. This new struggle wasn't kind to many in my industry.

That buddy of mine, Bart Burns, who had been a captain in the Marine Corps, went up and was interviewed for a part in a show. He got the part. By the time he got home they called him and said, "Bart, we're sorry, but we can't use you."

He said, "Well, I'd like to know why."

They said, "Well you just didn't meet the requirements."

He said, "What requirements are those?"

They told him they couldn't take him because he was not eligible under the new rules.

"What 'new rules'?" he demanded.

They explained that he had been hanging around with a few actors and writers who had an affiliation with communist causes. Mind you, they never said he was a communist himself. Only that he hung out with them.

Bart was furious. He went to the studio with his medals and his captain's bars from the Marines. He put those on the table and said, "Does this look like I'm a goddamn communist?"

They didn't answer. They still didn't use him.

In hindsight, it's easy to see how unjust these witch hunts were. At the time, no matter how much you hurt for the people who were affected, there was nothing you could do about it. I suppose it might have been different if everyone banded together and said we're not going to take it. But there were a lot of folks who believed in the cause, who were afraid of the Red Scare. It was just something that had to work itself out. In a way, that's one of the strengths of this country. No matter how far we swing one way or the other, the pendulum always returns to the middle. It's just too bad the human toll is always so high.

But you don't always realize you're in the middle of world-shaping events. Sometimes you're too busy trying to survive. I know I was. On stage, I got myself a job with the great Helen Hayes and Jules Munshin in a play called *Mrs. McThing*. Julie Munshin went on to play with Gene Kelly and Frank Sinatra in the movie version of *On the Town*, among many others. Also in the cast were Professor Irwin Corey, a very funny guy, and Fred Gwynne, who would go on to star as Herman Munster on TV.

One of the best things that ever happened to me occurred during the run of the show: my daughter Nancee was born. I'm sure that what I felt wasn't new, but it was new to me. I was now responsible for guiding and supporting a new life. That was a different kind of responsibility than any I'd had before. No new parent is ever quite ready for it. However, I did have one advantage that most people don't: Helen Hayes said to me, "I'm going to be the godmother."

When Miss Hayes spoke, no one argued. Anyway, it was a great idea. She became Nancee's godmother, remembering her on birthdays and holidays and writing her letters from the road. Miss Hayes took that role as seriously as she took every other one. I was glad for her interest because I had my hands full! I was working on Broadway and doing television work. Somehow I made enough money to support my little family. I was promised a certain fee, but the show wasn't getting the kind of advance sale they'd hoped so I got a pay cut. The way I found out was just plain lousy. Just before I was ready to make my entrance, one of the producers came over and said, "We can only afford to give you $125 a week. Take it or leave it. If you don't want the job, we've got your understudy waiting to go on."

Well, where the hell was I going to get $125 a week? I still had it better than my poor buddy Bart and I took the deal, but I swore that if I ever made good and worked for that bastard again I'd charge him a million bucks.

I learned a lot about the art and craft of acting from Miss Hayes, who had the kind of concentration that actors strive for. She could get into character in a heartbeat, and stayed there till the curtain came down. Then she was Miss Hayes again, charming and warm and great to be around.

Meanwhile, with plays running only a few weeks or my parts in them being relatively small, television proved to be my real bread and butter. My name was not well known but people in the street would occasionally look at me and say, "Didn't we see you on television?" It was nice to hear that. Unlike the theater, you worked in a studio, live but without an audience. It was nice to know people were seeing my work! I was doing okay, even if I wasn't Charlton Heston, who was the leading man in television at that time. Given his stature—six-foot-four—his chiseled good looks, and his sonorous voice, he was perfect for the new medium. He broke through that fuzzy black-and-white screen and tinny audio and in short order—by 1951—he made the same impact on the big screen. I had to wait a little longer.

The show that kept me going during this period was *Captain Video and His Video Rangers*. I owed that gig to a woman named Elizabeth

Mears, the casting director for the short-lived DuMont network. It was a raggedy thing, but it paid. If you worked every day you got $300 for the week. Captain Video, played by the square-jawed Al Hodge, zipped around in a jet, aided by super-advanced TV recon capabilities. He battled bad guys with futuristic-sounding names like Mook, Nargola, and Clysmok. One of his cohorts was played by Don Hastings, brother of Bob Hastings, who worked with me later on *McHale's Navy*. I played a variety of parts in the show, usually bad guys.

One of those bad-guy roles was Captain Neptune. They photographed me through a goldfish bowl to show the fish swimming by. I would go around with my mouth looking like a fish going, "wa wa wa wa." It was the craziest thing you ever saw. It was a popular show and when I'd come home at night the kids would throw stones at me because they watched the show that afternoon and knew who I was. That kind of recognition I could have lived without!

Talk about recognition. Let me tell you about Wally Cox.

The Copper was the name of a TV show I did with Wally. It was a *Goodyear Television Playhouse* episode and he was playing a New York cop. His character wanted to marry my character's daughter. Only problem was, I was in Sing Sing, where I was due to die in the electric chair. Somehow, Wally had to save my hide before he could marry my daughter.

Once we started rehearsing—which we usually had no more than a day or two to do—we realized we had to make numerous cuts to fit the slot. Delbert Mann was directing, and he was frustrated at how we were literally gutting the show. Finally, as airtime approached, he sighed and said, "Okay. Let's go ahead and see what the hell we can do."

Delbert continued to work on the script, and in all the confusion he forgot to tell us that not only were we going live, but we'd be seen coast to coast, for the first time. Back then, live shows were literally filmed off a television screen for viewing in other time zones. This meant we were going to be seen by at least twenty million people.

He added, "So give it all your best."

We finished that show with time to spare, enough so that we could do a complete crawl of credits at the end of the show. That didn't always happen.

Wally Cox was a funny little man. Most of you probably remember him from the Salvo laundry detergent commercials in the 1960s or later on the original *Hollywood Squares*. Back then, though, he was a real up-and-comer. He used to ride a motorcycle through Manhattan with his roommate and best friend, Marlon Brando. They made quite a sight, the scrawny Wally and the brooding Marlon pulling up to this diner or that theater. Marlon was appearing in *A Streetcar Named Desire*. They got a lot of press at the time. You need that to survive in this business, too.

Chapter 12

Escape to L.A.

We lived in South Queens for quite a while, near the ocean. One day my hand was hanging off the bed and I suddenly felt water there. The ocean had come up too high and we'd been flooded—no joke! We were practically underwater. So we got the hell out of there fast and found another place in Jackson Heights, not too far from the site of the 1939 World's Fair.

The new place was even worse. The woman upstairs wore the highest heels in America. She sounded like a big hailstorm every time she walked. Seven dogs lived in the apartment with her. When she left those dogs were by themselves, and the place stank. I was so mad I put my fist through the wall. It was a hellhole. I didn't want my wife and daughter living there.

But better days were around the corner.

Through the grapevine, I heard they were casting a picture called *The Whistle at Eaton Falls* and were looking for people. I decided to go to the production office and see what it was all about. I walked in like I belonged there—which was the only way to do it without an appointment—and asked the nice lady sitting behind a desk, "Do you think there'd be anything for me in this picture?"

She looked up and said, "Just a moment."

I thought she was going to get a security guy. Instead, she came back with a gentleman who had a thick German accent. Turned out he was the director. His name was Robert Siodmak, and he had made some great pictures, like *The Killers* with Burt Lancaster and Ava Gardner and *The Suspect* with Charles Laughton.

Siodmak looked me up and down and said, "You come see me tomorrow. I'll give you a screen test."

I was the very last person to be shot. By the time they got to me they were hurrying things along so it was "MOS," which in Hollywood lingo meant without sound. The original director who used the phrase was European, and with his accent it came out "Mitt Out Sound." Hence, "MOS."

Mr. Siodmak said, "Smile."

I asked him, "What should I say?"

Since there was no sound on the film, he said "Just say 'shit' over and over!"

Later, when the producer looked at my face on the screen he said, "Gee, he's got a nice smile. What's he saying?"

I'm told the director replied with a little smile of his own, "I don't know, but whatever it was made him smile."

When they called to tell me I'd booked the film, I thought I was going to do a couple of days' work as an extra. In fact, I was playing a featured role, the foreman of a factory. I was in some pretty good company: Lloyd Bridges, Dorothy Gish, Carleton Carpenter, Murray Hamilton, Anne Francis, and Arthur O'Connell, with whom I'd reteam twenty-two years later in *The Poseidon Adventure*. Not a bad way to start! Even though I was new to the medium, I understood how a camera worked thanks to my experience in television. I don't mean mechanically, I mean what it saw. For example, I had learned that if they were only shooting your face, you had to be expressive without using your hands. No one was going to see them. Likewise, I couldn't be as broad as I was onstage. The camera saw everything and then blew it up forty feet tall.

I must have done okay because I was asked to read for another movie after that, *The Mob*, starring Broderick Crawford. Unlike the Siodmak film, this one was going to be shot in Hollywood. I went to the casting call, saw the other actors, then walked over to the casting director, a man named Maxwell Arnow.

I said, "Do you mind very much if I don't watch the others, sir?"

He said, "No, no, that's okay. Just wait in the hall."

I walked out and sat on a hard wooden bench and waited. I wasn't being a snob or anything: I just wanted my interpretation to be fresh. I didn't want to be watching Mr. Arnow or anyone else as they reacted to things. Their expressions would color my own audition.

Finally, the last actor walked out and I was brought in.

I had noticed the position of the chair was different than when I'd come in. It had been sat in. I figured I'd do something different.

I said to Mr. Arnow and his panel, "Would you mind very much if I sat on the edge of the desk?"

"Not at all," Mr. Arnow said. "In fact, that's a good idea."

So I cleared a space and sat on the edge of the desk and I looked at an imaginary character as the script girl started reading the other lines off-camera.

During the course of the scene I leaned over and swatted the character that I was supposedly looking at, smacked him one across the puss. And I said the line—I'll never forget it—"Now, are you going to tell me or aren't you?"

When I finished, the director laughed and said "Okay, cut, print. I'll see you in Hollywood."

Two weeks later Arnow called and made it official. Leaving Rhoda and our daughter with her parents, I went west to play a union thug named Joe Castro. I hadn't been to Los Angeles since my navy days, and it had changed a great deal. The world markets had been partly closed to Hollywood during the war. Now they were open again, and everyone wanted Hollywood films. Studios, independent producers, and even the fledgling TV networks with their filmed half-hour crime shows and situation comedies were keeping soundstages humming.

I enjoyed working with Crawford, who had won an Oscar for *All the King's Men* the year before. He was a very nice guy personally, very unassuming, and he had an amazing photographic memory. I really envied him that. He could look at a page of script once, then turn around and do it perfectly.

I don't remember much else about the film, except that this intense, wiry kid named Charlie Bronson had a small, uncredited part as a longshoreman. Talk about paying your dues: it would be another ten years before he achieved stardom in a picture called *The Magnificent Seven*.

After finishing *The Mob*, Columbia wanted to get full value for their airplane ticket. So they put me in *China Corsair*, where I played Hu Chang, a Chinese shopkeeper. At four in the morning I used to show up at the makeup center in Columbia Studios on Gower Street and they'd put on adhesive strips to hold my eyes back. I wore them all day long. I could hardly see where the hell I was going, and when I sweated under those lights the tape had to be reapplied.

I remember one scene where I was supposed to go into the water. They had a stunt guy standing by, ready to jump in for me, but I didn't want any part of that. I was a sailor. I'd been in the drink before, as you may recall. So I jumped. Everybody hurried over to get me out before I drowned, but I was already climbing the ladder. They just thought that was tremendous, and Arnow wanted to give me a seven-year contract on the spot. The only catch: I'd have to move to Los Angeles.

I thought about that overnight and I knew it'd never fly. My wife would never come because she wanted to be close to her parents, who were in New York. When I politely—and regretfully—declined the offer, the head of Columbia Pictures, Harry Cohn himself, came down to the set to see me. He was every inch the ferocious Hollywood mogul, with his coat thrown over his shoulders (in those days that was con-sidered real chic, very European) and a couple of secretaries in tow. He glared at me and said, "We're going to give you $150 a week and you're going to make pictures for us."

I said, "Mr. Cohn, sir, I think that's wonderful and I appreciate it very much. But I can't take it."

"What do you mean you can't take it? How much are you making back in New York?"

"Well," I said, "in a good week I can make twice that in TV."

"How many good weeks do you have?" he asked without missing a beat.

"Not enough," I admitted with a grin. "But my wife is attached to her family and she doesn't like California. So what am I gonna do?"

"Is she Jewish?" he asked. Cohn himself was Jewish.

"As a matter of fact she is."

He snorted, "Damn Jews are all alike. When you're finished with this picture, get the hell out of here."

Wow, I thought. *There goes my movie career!*

After he'd gone, Arnow came over to me and said, "Listen, don't worry about it. He throws a lot of people off the lot until he needs them again. If something comes along, I'll have you back. Don't you worry."

I couldn't promise I wouldn't worry, but I thanked him very much. In retrospect, though, I'm glad I didn't take the deal. In those days they put contract players into everything, and you couldn't say no. It's true that they taught you all kinds of skills—riding, dancing, sword-play, all of that. But it was difficult to break out, especially with all the stars they had under contract.

Because *China Corsair* was a low-budget production, it actually came out before *The Whistle at Eaton Falls*—so, technically, that was my film debut. Thanks to Arnow, though, it wasn't my last.

Chapter 13

From Here to Eternity . . . and Beyond

It was 1952 and I was really starting to regret that I hadn't taken Harry Cohn's offer. The three movies hadn't set the world on fire and, ironically, more and more TV work was shifting to Hollywood, where there was a deeper pool of nationally known actors to draw from. The lack of opportunities left me a little depressed. That was when my old buddy Bart Burns saw a picture that he thought I ought to see.

We didn't have enough money for my wife to go to the movie with me, and we couldn't afford a babysitter, so I went alone. When I came back I was euphoric. I had seen Charlie Chaplin in *Limelight*. What a picture! It was a love story about an old comedian who couldn't get work, and a young ballerina whom he saves from committing suicide. It was so full of hope! That film was just the tonic I needed. I had work, we weren't living in the streets, and if I kept my shoulder to the grindstone things were bound to get better.

They did. Not long before I was ready to take a job at the post office, Max Arnow called.

He asked, "How soon can you get out here to Hollywood?"

I said, "Why?" It was a stupid question; it didn't matter. It was work and I needed some.

Arnow didn't know how unemployed I was, though, and actually tried to sell me on the project. He said, "They are interested in seeing you for the part of Fatso Judson in *From Here To Eternity*."

I almost dropped the phone. I had read the novel almost three years before. It was a massive tome, a huge best seller based on author James Jones's own war experiences at Pearl Harbor. At the time I remember thinking what a great part the sadistic jailer would be for me. I told Arnow I was free, but asked if they were going to be looking at anyone in New York. I wasn't trying to play hard to get. I needed to be here to earn a paycheck.

Arnow said that director Fred Zinnemann would be in New York and set up a time for me to go and see him. He told me to bring a monologue; anything, it didn't matter.

I honestly don't remember what I read. Truth be told, the audition was a total nothing. By that I mean I felt from the way he looked at me that he had made his decision when I walked in the door. Of course, I didn't know at the time what that decision was. And to tell you the truth, my heart sank a little when we started talking and he told me that Frank Sinatra was going to be in the picture as Private Maggio, the guy whose skull I would fatally crack in the stockade.

"My God," I thought, "they're making a musical out of it!"

I didn't know Frank at the time, but I figured anything he did was going to have singing and dancing in it. How wrong I was.

No sooner had I got home than the phone rang. It was Arnow.

"There's a ticket waiting for you at the airport," he said. "See you tomorrow."

Unlike my first three films, this was a big deal. Based on a hot book and filled with names like Montgomery Clift, Burt Lancaster, Deborah Kerr, Donna Reed, and of course, Mr. Sinatra. I was excited and, for the first time in a while, I was terrified.

This was the major leagues.

I got a place near Columbia Studio, a hotel that catered to struggling actors. When I reported to the studio the first thing I was told was to get a haircut. There was a barbershop around the corner, so I went and got a crew cut and came back.

"No, no, no," Zinnemann said. "Much shorter, much shorter."

I got a total of nine haircuts that day until Zinnemann finally approved.

Mind you, I had very little money at the time, so I went over to the first assistant director and said, "Who do I see about getting paid back for my nine haircuts?"

He said, "No one. You did that on your own."

I said, "No, I did it for the studio."

"Then you should have gone to the makeup department and had them do it," he said.

You live and learn. But years later, when I went back to Columbia for my first starring role in *Man on a String*, they asked how much I wanted for the film. I named my fee, then added, "That, plus the price of nine haircuts."

They said, "What?"

When I told them the story, they laughed. And Columbia finally paid for my haircuts.

Even before the cameras rolled, it was like being back in the navy. I don't just mean the short haircut. Producer Buddy Adler had to give final approval of how I looked. He wanted the movie to be true to life and true to the Jones novel. I stood outside the door with Henry Helfman, the gentleman who had dressed me.

As we waited, Henry looked at me kind of funny.

"Something wrong?" I asked. I was anxious enough and didn't need him fretting beside me.

He said, "It just doesn't look right."

"What doesn't?" I asked. "Can you be more specific?"

"Your stomach's too flat. Can you do something about that?"

That was the first time anyone had ever said anything like "you're not fat enough" to me! I said, "You mean like this?" and I pooched it out.

His eyes opened wide. "My God, that's perfect. Can you hold it?" I said, "Sure."

So we walked in. Buddy Adler took one look at me and said "Oh, my God, that's my Fatso Judson!"

I exhaled with relief. So did Henry. It was a great moment, and he and I are still buddies, fifty-five years later!

That first day of work I was sweating bullets—more than they fired during the course of the movie. Everyone was there. All the stars came that day to see the commencement of the picture. I was in full costume and was introduced as the guy playing Fatso Judson. They stared at me a couple of seconds before saying anything. Everyone had a lot riding on the success of this picture. Expectations for a world-class film and a big hit were high. If it flopped, all the big names would be splashed with mud. Burt's look was especially analytical. That was the way he was; the man studied everything in every movie he ever made. I'll talk more about him a little later. Finally, the ladies kissed me and the men shook my hand. They all seemed to approve.

I had rehearsed some with Frank, but I was scared stiff. It was a scene in the New Congress Club, a brothel in the novel but a kind of USO hangout in the film. I started playing the piano—faking it, as they'd taught me—when Sinatra's character looked up from the girl he was dancing with and said, "Why don't you knock it off, buddy, and put a mute in that thing?"

I stood up from the piano stool and turned to face him. The way the set was constructed, Sinatra was down in a sort of pit to make me look a little larger. As I stood up he said, "Jesus Christ, he looks ten feet tall!"

Everybody broke up, including me. We did the scene a few times until the director had what he wanted, but let me tell you—I swore allegiance and everything else to Frank Sinatra. All of my scenes in the film were with him, and a few with Monty and Burt. Frank was scared, too, he told me later. His film and recording career had kind of hit a slump and this was an important comeback film for him. Despite the pressure he was feeling, he did everything he could to make sure I was comfortable and that I looked good.

Monty and I got along pretty good. He didn't socialize much with the other actors, but he always knew his lines and was focused on the work. He just oozed sincerity in all his scenes, and that really helped me and the other actors get to the top of our game. Funny thing, but true: he was actually an inch taller than me, but the way he hunched over to suggest his character's basic shyness, you'd swear I had about half a foot on him.

One day we were sitting in an empty stage, running our lines and waiting to be called. We figured we had it down and put the work aside—you don't want it to get stale—and we started talking about where I came from, where he came from, and so on. He was really interested in my navy days. He had tried to sign up during the war but had been rejected for chronic diarrhea, of all things. And I was fascinated by his professional history: he'd made his Broadway debut at the age of thirteen and never looked back.

A door opened on the far side of the stage and this man and woman walked through. We didn't pay any attention because we were so into talking to each other. Suddenly I was embraced from behind by the man who had entered. He said in a deep voice, "You're absolutely the son of a bitch I wrote about."

It was James Jones, the book's author, and a PR gal from the studio. Mr. Jones congratulated me and said, "I didn't think we could have ever found anybody better than you. You're great. Keep it up."

Talk about an ego boost! Monty just smiled and winked at me. He knew what it meant.

Later on, Monty and I had to do our big knife-fight scene at the Columbia Ranch out in San Fernando Valley. They'd built a set to look like a back street in a small Hawaiian town. Zinnemann had been working with two stuntmen to stage the fight scene. When we arrived, he had them show us the moves—the lunges and slashes that would make it look authentic. It was a night scene, and we worked on it from four o'clock on a Saturday afternoon until five o'clock the following morning. We pushed and pulled and pounded and pretended to cut each other till we were black and blue. But we finally had a fight in the can.

At the end of it, after Monty had stuck his switchblade in my belly, I was supposed to say, "You've killed me. Why did you want to kill me?"

Well, I had literally been working on that line for seven weeks. If I didn't say it with the right mix of astonishment and horror—after all, I was supposed to be big and mean and he was supposed to be some punk horn player who didn't even want to box on the regimental squad—it was going to seem silly. I could just imagine some guy coming up to me after seeing the movie and kind of mincing, *"Oooo, you killed me. Why did you want to kill me, you bad boy?"* like I was a coward.

You never know how the public will take a line like that.

Well, cut ahead a few months. Back in New York, I went to see the movie for the first time at a private screening. As I watched Monty standing over me with that knife and staring down at me, I waited expectantly for the line, to see how it played with an audience. Well, it never came!

They had cut the line after all my work.

As I sat there boiling, I thought, well, of course they cut it. They left me the bad guy till the end. Had I said that line I might have sounded sad and sympathetic. By cutting that line they did me a favor. They made me the biggest heavy in Hollywood.

Cut ahead a year. I was back in Hollywood, and had gone down Ventura Boulevard to pick up a pizza. I made a big U-turn as I left the pizza place and suddenly I heard a police car behind me. Two officers approached the car. I guess they had seen that there was a big, tough-looking mug behind the wheel.

I took out my driver's license and said as graciously as possible, "What's the matter, officer?"

He said, "You can't make a U-turn from one side of the street to the other side."

I pointed to my license and said that I was from New York and didn't know that, but he didn't care.

So he took my license and looked at it, then he looked at me and looked at the license again, and he said to his partner, "Hey, Joe, guess what? I caught the son of a bitch that killed Frank Sinatra."

Being recognized didn't help me any. He gave me a ticket while he was laughing.

Back to the shoot. When we finished shooting the fight, Monty and I went up to his room, at the Roosevelt Hotel. We sat there waiting for Frank, who was supposed to show with booze and some broads but never even made it himself. Well, that was Frank. He was a great guy when you were around him, all kinds of fun and good humor— when you could pin him down.

So Monty and me, we sat there talking about cabbages and kings and watching the sun rise. It was the most interesting, inspiring, *fun* talk I've ever had with a man in my life. He was a wonderful, loyal, quiet, self-effacing young man with more talent than anyone I ever met. Years later, when I was told he was gay, I really was surprised. The only thing I could figure was that, if it were true, maybe he was having a problem coming out of the closet. That could also explain his alcoholism, which would take a heavy toll on him, both mentally and physically. In those days, coming out wasn't as easy as it is today. I mean, I worked with Rock Hudson years later on *Ice Station Zebra* and his homosexuality was a kind of big, open secret. Since Monty's not here to answer one way or the other, I'll leave it for others to speculate. He never made a pass at me, but maybe that was just me. All I know for a fact is that he died too young at the age of forty-five.

Before leaving the subject of *From Here to Eternity*, I want to mention one other actor who was in the movie: George Reeves. I was sorry

I didn't have any scenes with him. George had played one of the Tarleton Twins in *Gone With the Wind* and was on his way to becoming a big star when he went to fight in the war. By the time he returned, his window of opportunity had passed. He took low-budget movies and had spent a couple of seasons as TV's Superman before being cast in the key role of Stark in *From Here to Eternity*. Sadly, this was not to be his comeback, as he hoped it would. As soon as he came on-screen with that distinctive voice and profile, preview audiences said, "Hey, there's Superman!" His scenes were cut to a minimum and a few years later he put a bullet to the brain. Or so the story went. (Some claimed he was knocked off by a jealous woman. But either way, dead is dead.)

I don't know if it's this business and a life in the public eye that does strange things to people, or if actors as a lot are just more sensitive to emotional hardships than others. All I can say is that I feel blessed to have been pretty grounded throughout my life, something that comes, I think, from having been raised in a close-knit family that never judged me or made me feel odd or unwanted. They took Ernie Borgnine as he was, and for that I am more grateful than I can ever say.

Chapter 14

Go West, Young Family

No sooner had I finished *From Here to Eternity* and gone home to New York than, *bam*, I was asked to come right back again to shoot a western, *Stranger Wore a Gun,* with Randolph Scott, Lee Marvin, and Alfonso Bedoya, who had played Gold Hat, the head of the thieves who killed Humphrey Bogart in *The Treasure of the Sierra Madre.*

There was no such thing as frequent-flier miles in 1953, just loud, nine-hour trips by prop plane. They were wearing me out and, besides, it was clear that film was where my future lay.

I said to Rhoda, "Honey, you've got to make up your mind one way or the other, We should move out to Hollywood because they want to use me."

She agreed to go, but I sensed—and she did, too—that she was never going to be happy there. Still, she was a trouper for a while.

My first western proved to be a great experience. Alfonso was quite a character. He had these awful-looking teeth, but that was his character and it was one of the reasons why everybody used him. After we finished shooting, he went home to Mexico and got a complete new set of teeth. At the premiere, he said "Look at me. I got all my teeth fixed."

His agent, who was standing nearby, was horrified. "You dummy!" he yelled. "That is exactly what you're *not* supposed to do!"

The Stranger Wore a Gun was the picture where I met a lifelong friend, Lee Marvin. Rhoda was still back in New York and I was living at this hotel for men. The studio sent a stretch limo to pick me up for a location shoot in Lone Pine, California. When the car arrived, I had two great big suitcases, which they put into the trunk. I got into the stretch and saw this long-legged guy with a little overnight satchel and a funny look on his face.

He looked at me and he said, "What the hell's with the suitcases?"

I told him, "Well I can't leave them down here because nobody knows me and I don't know where to put them. I've got to go back to New York and pick up my family after the picture's over."

"Uh, huh," he said. He looked me over with those steely eyes of his. "You serve?"

I knew what he meant. "Navy," I replied.

He grinned. "I thought so, way you're all packed up for a long sea voyage."

I learned that Lee had been in the marines and those boys like to travel light. I also found out that he was wounded in the Battle of Saipan—shot in the ass by a bullet that severed his sciatic nerve. He used to joke that of course they put him in pictures like *The Wild One* or westerns where he had to ride.

"I can be kicked in the backside by a mule and I wouldn't feel it," he said.

We talked back and forth and we smoked back and forth. (I gave up the cigarette habit a few years later.) We were getting along pretty good by the time we reached Lone Pine.

The director was André De Toth, who wore an eye patch, having lost an eye as a kid. But here he was, directing a movie in 3-D! For those of you too young to remember, that was a short-lived craze where you put on cardboard glasses with red and green paper lenses that made it look like spears and lions and the Creature from the Black Lagoon were coming off the screen and right into your face.

When we arrived, Mr. De Toth looked at me with this kind of sideward glance and said, "You ride, don't you?"

I said, "Yes, sir."

I didn't, but I'd learned that you never said "No." That could cost you a job.

After we'd gotten into our costumes—I was playing a tough gang member named Bull Slager—Mr. De Toth said, "You see that man standing up there on that little hill?"

I said, "Yes, sir."

He said, "I want you to ride up there, turn your horse around, and when I drop the handkerchief, you come down here lickety-split, grab your gun out of your holster, say 'Take cover, men' and go out of the scene."

After surreptitiously watching how the other actors mounted their horses, I did the same and rode up to where some stuntmen were slipping and sliding on what little snow that was left. I rode slowly, because the snow was treacherous and there were boulders all over the place.

The horse got me where I needed to be, but when I turned around, what had seemed like a little hill now looked like a mountain, straight down. I must have looked a little green around the gills, because a wrangler nearby asked, "Ernie, what's the matter?"

I said, "Ah . . . I didn't expect the hill to be so steep."

He said, "Tell you what. Just give the horse his head, he knows what he's got to do, which is get down from here. If he drops his head any, just yank 'er up, because then he won't trip."

Sure enough, the handkerchief dropped and off I went. I had that horse's head in my lap all the way down. I came in with a flourish, yelling, "Take cover, men!" Then I drew my pistol, jumped off the horse, went out of the scene, and nearly fainted.

Randolph Scott came up to me, took off his spurs and handed them to me. "Kid," he said, "that was a helluva stunt. You earned 'em."

But I looked over where some of the crew was standing and there was Lee Marvin, wagging a finger and tsk-tsking. He gave me a kind of amused look that said, *I know you ain't no rider, but I'm not gonna rat you out.*

We became great friends. I have a picture of him dressed as the hobo in another film we did, *Emperor of the North*, and I asked him to sign it. He put down "To Ernie, love, Randolph Scott."

That rascal.

My next picture was a new experience for me. It was another western, *Johnny Guitar*—starring Joan Crawford, of all people, as the "Gun-Queen of Arizona"—and it was the first film I made for a studio other than Columbia. It was produced by Republic, a small operation, but there was nothing else in the offing and I wanted to work. Besides, it was being directed by Nicholas Ray, the brilliant young firebrand who made *They Live by Night* and *On Dangerous Ground*. After directing my film, he went on to do *Rebel Without a Cause*.

Along with Joan we had Mercedes McCambridge, Sterling Hayden, Royal Dano, and Ward Bond. We went out into the wilds of Sedona, Arizona, which was a tiny town in the fifties. It was an okay film, but the real drama was all behind the camera, where Nick Ray was playing both sides against the middle: both Joan and Mercedes were vying for his charms. To make things worse (or better, since it played well on screen) Joan hated Mercedes with a passion. She called her all kinds of insulting names, and poor Mercedes would fall apart. She'd literally go weak in the knees and collapse, she was that frightened of Joan Crawford. I'll never forget the day that she was supposed to shoot Joan. Joan just looked at Mercedes and the pistol practically fell out of her hands. But as I said, their unhappy relationship onscreen was really credible since neither woman was acting.

On one of the last days of shooting we finished early, so several of us went to look around the town. Things appeared to be pretty quiet, so we headed back.

As we were passing her trailer, Joan Crawford happened to open the door. Seeing us, she called out, "Hey, guys, how are you? Come on in, let's have a drink."

Well, you didn't refuse Joan and stay on her good side, so we went in for a drink. We were all talking back and forth. It got to be a pretty raunchy session with everyone telling jokes, even Joan.

Mercedes wandered in. Obviously wanting to bury the hatchet, Mercedes thanked Joan profusely for the gathering.

Well, Joan thought she was mocking her. Suddenly, that famous face darkened and she let fly a fusillade of insults like I've never heard, not even in the navy. We flew out of there in a hurry, Mercedes leading the way. I don't know if she ever recovered from that picture, but I can sort of guess who she was channeling when she did the voice of the possessed Linda Blair in the movie *The Exorcist*!

From Here to Eternity had sparked enough interest in me that I was able to get seen for a lot of parts. I wanted very much to play Pancho Villa in the Brando picture *Viva Zapata!* I read for it and. I don't know how close I came, but director Elia Kazan took Alan Reed instead. Alan had been around for quite a few years longer than I had and was terrific in the part. You win some, you lose some. At least I was in the arena. (And as for Alan, his name might not be familiar, but his voice earned him worldwide fame as a little cartoon character named Fred Flintstone.)

Speaking of which, next up for me was another big prestige film: *Demetrius and the Gladiators*, which was a sequel to a very popular film, *The Robe*. I had to try out with a whole bunch of guys to play head of the gladiator school. They let the crew pick, and the crew all voted for me. So I got the part, with Victor Mature and the wonderful Susan Hayward heading the cast.

It was a good experience—what boy, even one who was thirty-seven, didn't like playing with swords? It was even better because I finally had my family with me. By this time Rhoda had moved to California. We rented a little place across the street from Harry Carey, Jr. It was owned by Gene Autry. I remember thinking, the first night we were there, how often I'd watched the singing cowboy on the screen . . . and now I was living in his house!

"You did okay for yourself, kid," I chuckled to myself.

Susan Hayward was a doll—beautiful, funny, talented, about as un-affected as a superstar could be. Mature was all right. He had been a leading man for five or six years, most famously as Samson in the Cecil B. DeMille picture. He was pleasant and easy to work with, but I don't think he took movie acting all that seriously. He had started on the stage at the Pasadena Playhouse. And it's easy for stage actors to be a little cynical about movies. Instead of doing a show from start to finish, you do it in little pieces. You psych yourself up, the camera rolls for a few minutes, then you go back to your trailer or dressing room and read the paper. It's serious work, but if you screw up, you can do it over again. There isn't the same kind of pressure. A lot of actors don't enjoy film as much as they do the stage, but you get paid so much it's tough to say no. I think Victor was one of those guys. He also had a "me vs. them" attitude toward the studios, which I found out about a year later when we did a picture called *Violent Saturday*. Lee Marvin was in that one, too. One day, Richard Fleischer, the di-rector, asked if Mature would dive underneath a car. The actor said, "No way!"

Fleischer was a little taken aback. "What if we dig a hole under-neath there, would you dive then?"

"I'm not going underneath that car!" Victor replied.

He told me later that he refused because he had once done a scene for Columbia and broke his leg on a motorcycle. He wasn't compen-sated for it, so his attitude was to hell with them all—he wasn't doing anything dangerous.

Lee and I thought he was being a little prissy about it. I mean, this was a different situation for a different director and not really that dangerous. It's part of what an actor is supposed to do. But Victor had his own view, and I guess he was entitled to it.

That year, 1954, turned out to be a really busy one for me. I did some episodic TV—a fun little drama called *Waterfront*—and a rather forgettable film for Mr. De Toth called *The Bounty Hunter*. You know, when you're hot you like to cash in on the demand because you never know when it will fade. And I got to work with some of the greats to boot! The absolute highlight of that period was when I went down to a beautiful little place outside Mexico City called Cuernavaca to make a western about revolutionary Mexico called *Vera Cruz*. It's a place of eternal springtime. In later years that's where I also lived for a while with my second wife, Katy Jurado.

Vera Cruz starred Gary Cooper, Burt Lancaster, Jack Elam, Charlie Bronson, Denise Darcel, Cesar Romero, George Macready, and me. It was quite an event. They pulled out all the stops, renting a castle in Mexico City where you're not allowed to shoot anymore. We had to be very careful that we didn't break anything. We even had to make sure that the wheels of the stagecoach didn't ruin the stones of the old castle.

One day while we were shooting, Charlie Bronson and I ran out of cigarettes. We had time between takes, so we decided to go down to the local store and buy some Mexican cigarettes. They were a pretty harsh smoke, but that's how hard up we were.

We started out the gates and were going down the road on our horses when a whole truckload of soldiers went by, all armed. We said, "Hola. ¿Cómo esta usted?"—"How are you?"

We waved back and suddenly we heard "¡Alto!" which means "stop." So we stopped and turned around. They all had their guns leveled at us. We said, "What the hell is happening?"

It seemed that they were after some crazed politician who was trying to make a name for himself in Mexico, and wanted to declare a revolution. The way we were dressed, as bandits, they thought maybe we were part of his gang. We said, "No, no, no, *artistas, artistas,* we're artists. We're actors!" They came over to the townspeople and inquired about us. People confirmed our story, that we were filming a picture nearby, so we were saved. Scared the hell out of me, though. Charlie, too, I'm sure, though he was too tough and taciturn to ever admit it.

Jack Elam and I shared a room at the hotel in Cuernavaca. We had been told "Don't drink the water, whatever you do, don't drink the water." There was this bottle of water that was put in our room every day, by whom we didn't know. We used the bottle to scrub our teeth and wash out things. We didn't drink it at all. That wasn't much of a problem, since we were drinking beer mostly.

Anyway, one day, Jack and I were lying around the pool. I was watching a girl, half interested in what she was doing because she was working in our room. As I'm sitting there, she came out and filled the bottle from the spigot right outside the door.

I bumped Jack. "Hey, kid, look, this is the water that we've been rinsing out with!"

From then on, we didn't care anymore. If you're going to catch the *turistas,* you're going to catch it.

I got to know Gary Cooper pretty well on that picture. He was the kind of a guy who, when we were on location, instead of eating the food that was brought to him, would give it to these little Mexican kids. Then he'd go down and buy the food from the Mexicans and eat that food. He was giving them money on the side as well.

The very first day that I saw "Coop," as he preferred to be called, he was walking down the road with one of the most beautiful girls I've ever seen in my life. Looking up, I could see that same beautiful girl gracing a billboard.

I said to Jack, "Boy, this guy works fast."

Well, I honestly don't know what they did in private, but in public that six-foot-three legend was a perfect gentleman, an absolutely wonderful man. He never got excited, never got angry, never got flustered. If he flubbed a line or bumped into a prop he apologized to the actors and director and we did it again.

Burt Lancaster was a different sort of animal. He was always in motion, hurling himself around, jumping here and jumping there. He used to be a circus acrobat, and part of him still was. Good old Gary Cooper just took his time, easy does it, but not Burt.

I mentioned earlier that Burt was very analytical. I think he felt insecure about not having had much of an education, so he worked hard to understand everything. He questioned other actors about their choices, he questioned directors about their instructions, he questioned writers about their scripts. Some of that is a good thing. For Burt, it was an obsession. But I have to say: it worked for him. He gave some of the most memorable performances in movie history, and you can't knock success.

One day when we were between takes, Burt had his children with him. Jack Elam was walleyed and it gave him a very sinister look, perfect for playing villains and gangsters. Burt pointed to Jack and said to his children, "Look at that man—doesn't he have funny eyes?"

Jack didn't appreciate that too much. He and Burt got into a pretty nasty fistfight. Aldrich and Gary Cooper had to pry them apart.

Burt would also try to outdo Coop, and you just don't outdo Gary Cooper. One day I had a late call and the production office told me to ride in the car with Gary Cooper. I was going to sit in the front with the driver, give Coop his privacy, but he said, "No, no, no, you sit back here with me. Come on."

So I got in the back and we started talking. He looked at me for a while.

"You know," he said, "I sure wish I could act like you."

I said, "What do you mean? You've got two Oscars on your mantelpiece."

He said, "I just got those for saying 'yup.' What you do comes from life, from experience. It's real."

He explained that it's actors like me who make actors like him look good! Well, I sure didn't agree with his assessment of his talents then, and I still don't. He was one of the most brilliant actors I've ever worked with, and I've worked with some pretty good ones. Watch Gary Cooper in his pictures. He not only listens but also answers in tune with what he's hearing. That's the kind of acting that really makes sense to an audience and to other actors. He's not just spouting lines, he's giving an answer to your line. I still learn an awful lot when I watch one of his films. He's another one who, at sixty years old, had a lot of good work still to do when he left us.

Chapter 15

Good Day at Black Rock

One day while we were making *Vera Cruz*, along came Delbert Mann, with whom I had worked in New York doing live television. Delbert was going to make his first motion picture and was visiting our location to learn from director Bob Aldrich how to shoot outdoors. Back then, TV was mostly shot in black-and-white and in a studio. It's a real challenge to know exactly what kind of settings you need and where to put the camera, especially when you're filming a wide-screen movie. In 1954, TV images were nearly square, while more and more movies were being filmed in a format nearly three times as wide as it was high.

While he was there, Bob Aldrich asked if he could read the script. Delbert said, "Of course," so Bob read it.

At a party a couple of weeks later, I'm told that somebody asked Bob, "I hear you read the script of *Marty*. Who do you think could play that part?"

Bob answered, "I know only one man who could do it. Ernie Borgnine."

"Come on," the other person said. "He does nothing but kill people in pictures. This is about a lonely butcher!"

Bob said, "Don't kid yourself. This guy can act."

The guy Bob was talking to was Harold Hecht, the producer of *Marty*. When I finished up in Mexico, I went back to Hollywood to prepare to make a picture with Spencer Tracy and Lee Marvin called *Bad Day at Black Rock*. Shortly before I left for the location, I got a call from Hecht to come and see him.

"Listen," he said, "we've heard some nice things about you from Bobby Aldrich and Delbert Mann. We've got a part for you in a picture called *Marty*."

I said, "Gee, that's wonderful. I would be very happy to play any part at all."

He said, "You don't understand. We're considering you for the lead."

I went absolutely blank for a moment as the words seeped into my brain. I didn't say "thanks" or "great, call my agent." What came from my mouth was "You have faith in me?" Because what Hecht had told Aldrich at the party was right: I was known for playing heavies.

He said, "Of course I have faith in you. Otherwise I wouldn't ask you."

I said, "That's all I wanted to know. Mr. Hecht, I'll give you 110 percent."

Hecht told me that writer Paddy Chayefsky and Delbert would fly up to Lone Pine where we were shooting, so that I could read for them. But after meeting me, he said he was pretty sure I'd get the part.

As I walked from his office with a bounce in my step, I looked up to heaven and gave a silent prayer of thanks. I hoped my mom was watching.

Bad Day at Black Rock is about a one-armed man who comes to a small town in the southwest to give a Japanese farmer his son's war medal. Director John Sturges—who went on to make *The Magnificent Seven* and *The Great Escape*—was a very nice man and a thoughtful director. He was always dragging on a cigarette, thinking hard about what we were about to do. I'll never forget when we were on location up at Lone Pine and we were supposed to do a scene where Spence and I had it out. I said to Mr. Sturges, "You got a guy with one arm. How's he gonna fight a big strapping guy like me when I'm throwing two arms?"

He said, "I was thinking about that myself. What do you suggest?"

I said, "What about judo?" That was something they'd taught us in the navy.

He said, "Okay. Work it out with the stunt guys."

Spence's stuntman and I started playing around with it, with input from my double. I knew enough judo to get by, but these guys knew what would look dramatic on a big screen. Spence was there, watching the entire time to learn the choreography, and so was Sturges. When we had something that looked like it could work, Sturges said, "Okay, we're gonna shoot it."

I stepped back so the stunt guys could fight. Sturges said, "No, no, you're in the shot."

I said, "Wait—can we work on it a little more?"

Sturges said through a cloud of cigarette smoke, "I want it a little rough and raw. Let's go!"

I thought, "Jesus Christ, I'm gonna get killed here." See, there's a famous story about how Spencer Tracy had once thrown a punch at Clark Gable in a picture called *Boom Town*. While Clark was zigging instead of zagging, Tracy hit him one right in the kisser and knocked out his front teeth. Tracy never threw another punch after that except close up.

But, no—the stunt double was going to be throwing me around. So we started the fight scene, which was taking place inside. I had this sponge full of stage blood hidden in my hand. He hit me and then he came up with his knee and just missed, on purpose. I went down then got back up, squeezing the sponge. You could see the blood spurt onto the ground.

I heard Spence say, "Jesus Christ, they killed him."

Fortunately, we were shooting this MOS. The grunts and cracks would be added later. Anyway, I came back and threw a punch at him. He gave me the judo flip we'd rehearsed and I hit this screen door just as I was supposed to. Except for one thing. During rehearsals, the screen door opened and I fell out onto an off-camera mattress. When we got to the actual fight, somebody had closed the screen door and latched it. I can still see in my mind's eye the hinges coming out as I hit that son-of-a-bitch going ninety-seven miles an hour. I want to tell you man, *bam!*

I just lay there. I moved my fingers and toes.

"Well, shit," I said, "it doesn't feel like I broke anything except the door."

I got up slowly and I was dizzy, then I threw a punch and got tossed upside down, and the scene was over. Then I remembered, because there was Lee Marvin, off camera, going "tsk, tsk, tsk."

That son of a bitch, I thought with a little chuckle. But he wasn't the biggest SOB. Five years later, when Sturges was shooting *The Magnificent Seven* in Cuernavaca, where I was living with my wife Katy Jurado, I went to the location to say hi.

During a break, I said, "John, I really want to know—who closed that darn door?"

He said, "I did."

I said, "You bastard."

He said, "I knew you could take it and I wanted it to look real."

If he'd been there, I'm sure Lee would've gone "tsk, tsk, tsk."

Everyone who's ever worked with Spencer Tracy has only nice things to say about him, and there's a reason for that. He was a giving actor, an unassuming star, and a real gentleman. He took his work seriously, but not himself. I asked him if it was true, as Hollywood legend had it, that his Best Actor Oscar for *Boys Town* had accidentally been inscribed, "Dick Tracy." He said it was and said it still made him chuckle. I remember thinking at the time that if I ever had the

outlandish good luck to win an Academy Award, they damn well better get my name right. But Spence was just so professional. He rarely
flubbed a line or missed a mark. If you screwed up, he was never impatient. If he screwed up, he got tight and quiet and made sure he got
it right the next time. As with Coop, you were on the top of your game
working with him. He listened, he reacted exactly right to whatever
lines you said to him, and as a result you looked real, natural—better.
That back-and-forth was like a tennis match where everything was
going right.

As planned, Delbert Mann and Paddy Chayefsky flew up to Lone
Pine. I went to their motel room straight from the set one night. They
gave me the script and told me what to read and I went right at it.

"Wait," Delbert said. "You're reading it with a western accent!"

Goddammit, I thought. Now there's a helluva first impression. I
stepped out of my boots, shed the big ten-gallon hat, and started over.
I was reading the part where I'm talking to my mom in the kitchen of
our apartment. I forget which one of them fed me the mom's lines,
because all I saw was my own mother standing there. I read the scene
and stopped.

Delbert and Paddy both had tears in their eyes.

Son of a gun, I said to myself. *I've got the part!*

Chapter 16

Several Close Calls

When it was announced that I was going to star in *Marty*, everybody in town—including some of the most powerful columnists, couldn't believe they'd hired me to play a lovable butcher.

Talk about pressure!

I proved them wrong, but there's a lesson in all this. Hollywood's got an awful lot of good actors who are just waiting for an opportunity to work in front of a camera. Those opportunities are few and far between and a lot of that has to do with preconceptions. Someone walks into an audition and some casting director immediately pegs him or her as a "Will Smith type" or a "Julia Roberts type." That can be good, if that's what they're looking for, or that can be bad. My attitude has always been: let the gal or guy read their lines and give it to them on merit alone. The public is pretty open-minded. If you do a good job, they'll accept Donna Reed as an "escort" in *From Here to Eternity* or Tyrone Power as a carnival freak in *Nightmare Alley*.

Or Ernie Borgnine as a lovable butcher.

One person I haven't mentioned in this process so far was Burt Lancaster. In that analytical brain of his, Burt had figured out what a lot of actors didn't realize until later: you had more control over your career

if you produced your own films. So he teamed with Harold Hecht—who
had discovered him—and writer James Hill and formed Hecht-Hill-
Lancaster Productions. In addition to *Marty*, which was their first film,
they went on to make *Separate Tables*, *The Sweet Smell of Success*, and
a bunch of other great pictures. Burt also had a say in the casting of
those movies, and his was a strong voice in favor of casting me. See,
Burt was a New York kid and he felt that the part of a New York
butcher had to be played by someone who'd lived there. He was also
a smart businessman: he knew that casting someone against type was
bound to get a lot of publicity, which it did. Even before we shot a
frame of film, people were eager to see the movie.

We shot *Marty* at Goldwyn Studios in Hollywood and on the streets
of New York City. Betsy Blair was playing Clara, the plain-looking
schoolteacher with whom Marty falls in love. Delbert took us and a
couple of the other actors to New York, where we rehearsed in a dance
hall on 48th Street. Delbert had no intention of spending any more
time in Hollywood than he had to.

Delbert had worked out all the moves like he used to do for television. He laid out the interior of the house and the other sets. By the
time we got to Hollywood, the sets were familiar to us and we were
able to shoot the picture in eighteen days.

That's just over two weeks to shoot a feature film! It was a lot of
work, but it was also good for the actors: we pretty much stayed in
character the whole time. When you weren't acting and learning lines,
you were sleeping.

I'll never forget when we had to dub the scene where I'm walking
along the street, talking to Betsy. You couldn't hear our dialogue because of the noise from the elevated subway. I did the whole speech
in one take. When we got through, Delbert just shook his head in
amazement. There was no "take two." I'd given him exactly what he
wanted, every letter absolutely perfect. The thing is, it was hell later
on when I had to dub all that dialogue in the recording studio. Lip-
synching is the hardest thing in the world. Not only do you have to

summon all the emotions you felt during the shoot, you have to pay close attention so what you're saying matches the lip movements. It's a bear, let me tell you. The one good thing about it is you get a chance to improve on things a little without the pressure of having the crew standing around burning up thousands of dollars an hour.

There were some memorable moments during the filming. We were filming up around Gun Hill Road in the Bronx. I was staying at a hotel in Manhattan, so they sent a car for me. The driver kind of looked at me funny, but didn't say anything. I figured he was used to driving actors around and was playing it cool. Anyway, it was only the second day of shooting. I got out and asked Paddy Chayevsky and Delbert Mann how the previous day's shooting went. By now they would have seen the rushes—the unedited film of all the takes from the previous day—and I figured they'd have some reaction. Directors usually did. But Delbert just said, "Oh, it was fine." Their reticence was probably a good idea. If they had any tweaks it was better to give them on the set, during the performance. If they made generalizations, like saying I was too broad or too mushy, I might overcompensate and go too far in the other direction.

Anyway, I went to the trailer where they had my dressing room and changed my clothes. I started walking back and forth outside, in the street, to soak in the atmosphere of Marty's world. Suddenly I felt a tap on my shoulder. I turned to see my driver and a bunch of guys standing there.

One of them said, "Hey, are you the guy who killed Frank Sinatra?"

I said, "Yes, that was me, Fatso Judson."

He said, "Yeah, well what'd you want to do that for?"

I said, "Well, you know, it was a picture. Just a movie."

Somebody spoke up, in Italian, in the background, "*Battiamo l'inferno da lui*"—"Let's beat the hell out of him."

Naturally, understanding Italian, I said, "*Giudichilo di destra là, il mioamico*"—"Hold it right there, my friend." That caught him a little off guard. I said, "Look, I happen to be Italian myself, and Frank and me, we're actually good friends. But, you know, if you guys want to start something, I'll take you on one at a time. I'm not afraid." They could tell I wasn't bluffing. In my head, I half-pictured Burt Lancaster—a scrapper himself—delighted at the press we'd get.

They said, "You're Italian? Borgnine?"

I said, "Yeah! It was Borgnino before my family changed it."

"Oh, my God," one of them said, "why didn't you tell us that?"

From then on I was getting pizza brought to me on the set every day. I had gallons of wine delivered to my dressing room. Dinners were on the house at local restaurants. Man, I tell you, we had a feast every day while we were shooting up around Gun Hill Road.

All the while, though, one holdout continued mumbling, "I still think we ought to beat the shit out of you for what you did to Frank Sinatra."

I learned a very valuable lesson from that experience, as humorous as it was. Never underestimate the power of the movies—these guys really believed I killed Sinatra. Seeing, to some people, really is believing.

We came back to Hollywood to finish shooting the film, but there was a problem.

No sets.

Everybody was stunned, especially Delbert, who had been told that they were being built. Turns out there were some financial shenanigans attached to the picture. The plan, I later learned, was to shoot half the movie, then put it on the shelf and write it off. That way, the producers could pay themselves a salary, yet not have to show a corporate profit.

But the tax man said no. In order to do that, they had to finish the picture, show it once, and *then* take a loss.

I'm not sure that was good news, but it was better news. We'd get to finish the film.

The producers spent a total of $273,000 making the picture. My salary was $5,000, with the promise of $5,000 more if I signed a seven-year contract with Hecht-Hill-Lancaster. They made that offer before I knew about the game they were playing and I signed. I figured that these guys were making quality films and I'd get to do more than play gunmen in westerns. As it turns out, I never did do a film for them and I never got the extra five grand either.

One day, a few months later, Burt Lancaster had just come back from shooting *The Kentuckian*, his one and only picture as a director. I remember him joking at the time, "I've been accused of directing films before. Now I can be blamed." It was actually a good movie and the screen debut of Walter Matthau—as a villain! Talk about playing against type.

Anyway, Burt asked if I wanted to see *Marty*.

Did I? You bet! I had a lot riding on the film. Whatever its fate, Hollywood has a very active grapevine. People would hear about my work, good or bad.

The screening room was very quiet with just me, my wife, and her mother—who had come to California to stay with us—and several others, including Burt Lancaster and Harold Hecht. We watched the picture and it seemed to play well. Everyone was attentive and, when it was over, they were complimentary. Me? I can't stand watching myself in motion pictures because I get scared that people will never want to pay good money to see my puss. But at the end, even I felt we'd done a pretty good job.

I didn't realize what we really had until I saw Burt Lancaster get up and motion for Harold Hecht to follow him. They walked to a corner of the room, where Burt picked him up by the front of his blazer, held him against the wall, and said, "This is the movie you weren't going to finish? Why the hell didn't you shoot *more?*"

Burt was enthusiastic about the film, and they put the publicity in the hands of Walter Seltzer, who later went on to become a producer, making some of Chuck Heston's most popular films, including *The*

Omega Man and *Soylent Green*, among many others. He took the picture and held invitational screenings to which he invited bootblacks, barbers, and manicurists—ordinary working folks who he thought would like the picture and talk it up to their friends and coworkers. Little by little, word got around.

Then he took it to New York and he started showing it to the critics. When it opened, everybody on busses, in restaurants, at ballgames would be asking each other, "Hey, have you seen *Marty?*" Speaking of ballgames, Joe DiMaggio went to see *Marty* with the rest of the New York Yankees. Everybody said, "Boy, oh boy, this is great." It was a sensation with lines around the block, the little movie that could! Back in Hollywood, the producers were making a fortune. Guess they didn't mind paying the taxes on that.

The distributor, United Artists, was also very happy with me. I started winning all kinds of awards. I won the Golden Globe. I went back to New York to get the award given by all the New York Film Critics.

It was quite a picture for me, but the best was yet to come.

Chapter 17

Oscar and Me

Here are a bunch of names and pictures for you to consider. James Cagney in *Love Me or Leave Me*.

Frank Sinatra in *The Man With the Golden Arm*.

James Dean in *East of Eden*.

Spencer Tracy in *Bad Day at Black Rock*.

And last, but to my mind least, Ernest Borgnine in *Marty*.

Those were the nominees for the Best Actor Oscar for the year 1955. As you know, I'd worked with Spence in *Bad Day at Black Rock*, and he did a great job. I was a fan. Poor James Dean had died in a car crash just a few months before. And Frank—jeez, all I had to do was beat him and those guys from the Bronx would come west and try to beat me.

Not that I thought there was any chance I would win.

You know, it's a couple of weeks between the time the Oscars are announced and the awards are given. You get a nice certificate saying you're a nominee and, as I said earlier, it really was flattering to be nominated. I mean, look at that company! But winning was out of the question, and that made it easy for me to weather the wait. Reporters who interviewed me were very complimentary about the film but, like me, they figured I didn't have a prayer of winning.

On the day of the Oscars I arrived for an early rehearsal. Who knew if I'd ever get there again as a nominee? I wanted to drink it up. Jerry Lewis was the master of ceremonies, and I met Grace Kelly for the first time. A couple of people said to me, "You're going to win, you're going to win," and I knew they were just being kind. I was sure they said the same thing to Spence and Jimmy.

Jerry Lewis was one of the yea-sayers, and he and I made a bet. At this point I should probably interject something about the Oscars. Yes, they're about merit. Merit is what gets you nominated. After that, though, prior history and playing against type and who you have or haven't pissed off in this town do hold some sway. So Jerry was not off base when he said, "Tracy's already won, Cagney's won, Frank won, and James Dean is gone. I'll bet you a buck ninety-eight that you're going to win."

Why a $1.98? I have no idea, you'd have to ask Jerry.

I said, "Okay." I went home and counted out 198 pennies and put them in my daughter Nancy's red sock. I came prepared to lose. If anyone saw the sock, I'm sure they would've thought I intended to clobber the winner with my improvised blackjack.

I went home and fell asleep that afternoon. I'll never forget Rhoda coming into the den and screaming at me, "How can you fall asleep? How can you sleep when you're up for an Academy Award?"

I said, "Why think about it? I'm not going to win, but I *am* going to be up late."

She was so mad she could have hit me with a rolling pin. Well, it was time to get dressed, anyway. I had the worst set of tails, too small, too hot, and a little ratty, but it was the last set the rental place had. We drove ourselves in a secondhand Cadillac I had just bought. We parked and walked to the Pantages Theatre on Hollywood Boulevard, where the Oscar ceremony was being held. We got to the theater just in time to see Clark Gable and his wife come in. Naturally everybody had to take a picture.

My wife, who was rather stout, said, "Oh, no."

I pulled her over and said, "Come on, get in here." So she hid herself behind me a little bit and we took a picture.

When we were done, Gable looked at me and winked and said, "You're going to make it."

I said, "Thanks a lot, Mr. Gable." I was thrilled to death just being in his company, let alone hearing such praise. I was still flying high from that as we took our seats.

Burt Lancaster was across the aisle from me, a couple of seats up. As we sat down he turned and said, "How are you?"

"Good," I said.

"That's fine," he said and smiled knowingly. It was as if he knew I was going to lose and was trying to let me down gently.

Finally, the time came for the Best Actor Award to be named. My poor wife was nervous, but I was sitting there rather placidly. It wasn't an act. I knew I wasn't going to win.

Suddenly, my wife was punching me in the side, saying, "They called your name, get up! Ernie, *they called your name!*"

I said, "What are you talking about?"

"You won!"

Man, I guess I'd gone off to la-la land. What a way to come back!

I got up and I gave a kiss to her and I saw Burt Lancaster look at me as if to say, "I don't know how the hell you did it, but it's yours!"

I walked up and naturally Jerry Lewis came to the steps. I handed him the red sock, paying him off, a buck ninety-eight. He later said he tossed the sock but invested the money and made a small fortune.

Then Grace Kelly came over and handed me the Oscar. Well, what could I say? I couldn't say very much anyway because I had nothing prepared. I knew I wanted to pay tribute to my mother and dad. My mom, especially, who stood between me and the relatives and folks in the neighborhood when they asked, "How come he's down in the cellar practicing? What is this stuff? Why doesn't he get a job and get married?"

I don't remember what else I said. I'm sure there's a film of it somewhere, but I never wanted to see it. If I didn't want to see myself doing lines in a film, I certainly didn't want to see myself tripping over my tongue on TV.

Later that night—it had to be about four in the morning on the East Coast—I called my father and asked, "Did you hear?"

He said, "Hell, yeah! And you know something? The first sons of bitches through the door were the guys who always said 'Tell him to get a job and settle down.' Now they were saying 'We knew he could do it.'"

Dad admitted he hadn't been to bed that night. He was celebrating with the rest of the family and hoping I'd call. I could tell he was just so proud of me. The only thing we regretted was that my mom wasn't there to share this with us.

Oh, and I heard through channels that the guys in the Bronx were pretty proud of me. No hard feelings there.

But I got my acting award and it sits up there on top of the television set in my home. I'm very proud of it because it shows that my peers thought well of me. The thing I'm still most proud of is that there have been very few character actors to win the Best Actor award. Mostly, it's leading men . . . and no one would ever mistake me for one of those!

Yet, thanks to *Marty* and my Oscar, I got to play a wider variety of parts than I ever dreamed of. Though not right away.

I had occasion to meet Kate Hepburn shortly after the Academy Awards. I was on the Twentieth Century-Fox lot and went over to thank Spencer Tracy for sending me a congratulatory telegram. He was shooting *Desk Set* at the time and was preparing to start *The Old Man and the Sea* not long after. I knocked on the door of his dressing room and he answered.

"Hey," he said, "I sent you a wire and you never even answered."

Kate poked her head from behind his shoulder and said, "Well, hell, he won the award, not you."

They invited me in and we had a lovely chat about what they were doing and what I was doing. I was a little embarrassed that I didn't have a prestige picture in the lineup. See, I had already been committed to several other pictures, mostly supporting roles, before *Marty* so I really hadn't been able to capitalize on the success. Spence gave me some good advice: he said, "Don't worry about trying to cash in. Just keep doing good work and the good parts will come."

He was right, of course. No matter how good you are, or how much attention you're getting at a particular time, you always run the risk of being last year's hot commodity, yesterday's flavor. Truthfully, when I thought back to being unemployed, I felt blessed to be getting as much work as I was.

A couple of months later, I was playing golf with columnist Jim Bacon and this guy came running up with a telegram. It was from my agent. It said that I should stand by to go to Cuba to replace Spencer Tracy in *The Old Man and the Sea.*

I asked Jim what the heck that was all about.

"Hemingway's working on the picture, too," Bacon said. "He's not happy with Tracy. Thinks he looks like a rich Hollywood guy and not a fisherman."

Apparently, the author thought I'd be better for the part. Well, there was no way in hell I was ever going to replace Spencer Tracy in anything and I said so. Hemingway shut his trap, the picture was finished, and Spence got himself another Oscar nomination.

Chapter 18

A Piece of No Action

Not every actor needs all kinds of managers and handlers. But one thing they do need, if they can get it, is a good agent. I haven't had a lot of luck there. Most of what I got, I got on my own.

I didn't have an agent when I started out and it was a bear to get into a lot of auditions. With agents, they just make a phone call and you're in. And not at six in the morning, when you'd have to go to sign up for an audition, go home, then come back later in the day. Agents can get you nice spots in the afternoon.

They're also—if they're good—pretty fearless. An actor might be afraid to say no to a low fee for fear of losing a part. Agents have no such qualms. Also, if they can't build you into a top moneymaker, they're not going to make enough at 10 or 15 percent for you to be worth their while.

Unless, of course, they have so many clients that a little from many is the same as a lot from one. For a while, I was stuck in that former situation.

Paul Wilkens was my agent because he had offices in New York and Hollywood, so he had first crack at whatever was being developed on either coast. I was also his first client to win an Academy Award, yet he didn't know what to do with me.

After *Marty* he continued to take what little money I'd been offered as before. He was satisfied, but I wasn't. I left him and went to somebody else, but it was all just the same mishmash with a different spin.

One time this producer/writer approached my agent and said, "I've got to get ahold of Borgnine. I want him for my picture."

My brilliant agent said, "What picture?"

He said, "I'm gonna make *The Shoes of the Fisherman*, a great big thing all about the Pope and the Vatican."

My agent said, "You can't have Borgnine."

"What do you mean I can't have him?"

"If you want him, you've got to take six other guys with him." See, this was that agent's way of using me to build the rest of his stable.

The producer, rightly, said, "I don't want six other guys. All I want is Borgnine."

My agent said, "Well, he's busy."

Morris L. West, the distinguished author, saw me later and said, "Dammit, what the hell's the matter with you?"

I asked him what he was talking about. He told me what my agent had done. I said, "Mr. West, I never even heard about this offer!"

Anthony Quinn got the part, and the opportunity to work with an amazing cast that included Laurence Olivier and John Gielgud. I was heartsick. I lost all faith in agents. Signing with the renowned William Morris Agency didn't bring it back. One of the heads of the agency said to his team—with me in the room—"I want the best for this man, because he's a wonderful actor."

Everybody said, "Yes, sir!"

So they assigned a hotshot agent to me for one solid year. I kept asking, "When do we get working?"

This guy would say, "We're looking for the greatest part in the world for you to start our relationship with."

I said, "I don't want the greatest part in the world. All I want to do is work so I can make enough money to feed my family."

He said, "Okay, Ernie, I'm on it."

I left William Morris after a year. I got my own jobs through networking and still had to pay them a commission. Unless you're on their tail all the time, unless you're working on something high profile that keeps you in the trades and in their faces, you're on the back burner.

Funny but true: the one job they *did* get me was for a big picture that was supposed to come with a big paycheck. That movie never got made.

That's why, if you remember back, I took the deal with Hecht-Hill-Lancaster.

Unfortunately, as I said, that didn't work out. What happened there was Burt was in New York filming *Sweet Smell of Success*—a brilliant film, one of the best American movies ever. Lancaster said there was a part for me in the film. I said okay. It was going to be an important film, about the corruption of a powerful newspaper columnist, loosely based on Walter Winchell. Tony Curtis was playing the suck-up who was always trying to get his clients in Lancaster's column.

That was late in 1956, seven months after the Oscar win, and I really wanted to be in another prestige picture. So I went to New York with my business manager to get the script from the headwaiter at the 21 Club. What he was doing with it, I have no idea. Maybe because they'd been shooting there they left it with him when they went to some other location. I don't know. Anyway, he gave the script to me.

My manager and I went back to my hotel. I read the script and found I had about twelve lines. They were damn good lines. I'd be playing a corrupt police detective.

Well, my manager absolutely wouldn't let me do the part. He said Hecht-Hill-Lancaster was using me, putting me down. We returned to Los Angeles, where the producers' attorneys informed me I was being put on suspension for breach of contract.

I was sick over that, and tried to figure out something that would lift my spirits. An idea hit me. I said, "Christmas is around the corner. I want to go to the five and dime, get a job selling things."

My manager and my wife both said, "You can't do that!"

I said, "Why not?"

"Because it would leave a bad impression."

"Bad impression?"

"It would look like you can't get work."

"Well," I said, "unless I work things out with Hecht-Hill-Lancaster and go out hustling, I won't get work. Not in my business. So, what the hell, I'll go to a five and dime. That'll probably get some publicity and maybe an offer for a picture."

They talked me out of it, but I still think it would've been a good thing to try. Something different. For me, "different" ended up being basically running my own career without all kinds of representatives. And thanks to guys like Lee Marvin, who always brought me in on movies he was working on, and directors like Robert Aldrich and John Carpenter who just got a kick out of my work, I've done okay.

Chapter 19

Talkin' Pictures, Part One

Now we can get back to the reason many of you are probably here: my film career.

Picking up in 1955, right after *Marty*, I'm going to run through so I can give you the highlights. Some of them were hits that you'll probably remember; some of them were turkeys that I barely remember. But even in those, there were people and places that stand out all these years later.

 ### Run for Cover

Acting with James Cagney was a special treat. He was so easy to work with. He did his work, knew his lines, and winked at you as we went along, to show that everything was fine. In the evening, when we'd finish, people would congregate around his dressing room. After he'd changed, he'd bring out a little square piece of wood and tap-dance on it. Everybody would hum a tune and he'd dance like crazy.

I only had a small role in the film, but it was more expensive to send me back from the New Mexico location than to put me up, so I stayed the whole shoot and enjoyed several weeks of free entertainment!

 ## *Violent Saturday*

I almost killed one of my best friends making this movie.

I was playing an Amish farmer. Lee Marvin and a crew of desperados were holding my family hostage in our barn. They tied us up, along with Victor Mature.

In one dramatic scene I was supposed to stab Lee Marvin in the back with a pitchfork. While we were rehearsing, they put a big X on his back. I was supposed to put the tines of the pitchfork right on this X, which was padded underneath so he wouldn't be hurt.

We rehearsed it fine, but when it came time to shoot, they'd removed the X so it wouldn't show.

I said, "Lee, I'm not sure about this."

He said, "I have faith in you. You'll hit it."

I said, "That's nice, but what if I miss?"

"Don't miss," was all my tough-guy pal said.

I didn't, but I was sure nervous when it came time to poke him. I mean, you've really got to put your muscle into it, or it's not going to look real. Later, instead of the usual "Tsk, tsk," he complimented me on my marksmanship.

"Just out of curiosity," he said, "what were you thinking about when you did that?"

"Well," I said, "I caught sight of myself in the beard and overalls and I imagined I was John Brown—a fellow Connecticut native, as it happens—at Harpers Ferry fighting off the soldiers of Robert E. Lee."

"My" Lee, Lee Marvin, said he was glad I hadn't told him that before or he'd have been scared stiff.

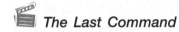 ## The Last Command

I have to say, they may not have been highfalutin, but there was nothing I had more fun doing than westerns. This one had Sterling Hayden and Slim Pickens, among others. It was a retelling of the battle of the Alamo, and Sterling Hayden was a great Jim Bowie. I died with a bayonet stuck into me, in a pool of my own blood. It was a pretty dramatic death—but they cut it out because the picture was too long.

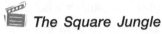 ## The Square Jungle

This movie is another reason that exclusive contracts are no damn good.

After signing that crappy deal with Hecht-Hill-Lancaster, we squared things away by having them loan me out. That meant they told any studio that wanted me to pay, say, $100,000 of which I got to keep roughly a quarter.

So along came *The Square Jungle*, which starred Tony Curtis. I played a fight manager. Despite the fact that I was getting ripped off, we had a lot of fun. An actor by the name of David Janssen in the film—kind of big ears, looked like Clark Gable—took me aside one day and he said, "I sure wish I could talk to you."

I said, "What's the matter? Talk to me."

He said, "I've got a contract here with Universal, but I'm not happy."

I laughed. "I want to tell you something. You've got a contract with a company that puts you in pictures. You may not be satisfied with what pictures you're getting, or the pay, but you're working and you're sharpening your tools as you go along. You know, they're selling me down the river, and I've won an Oscar. I'm hanging in there. You should, too."

Janssen said, "Maybe you're right. I'll stick around. I'm going to work hard."

Sure enough, one day he got that TV series *The Fugitive* and became Number One on the hit parade. Not long after that I happened to pull up alongside him on Wilshire Boulevard, sitting in his Rolls Royce. I was sitting in my little old Mercedes and I said "Hi, David, how are you?"

He said, "Oh, hi," and roared off.

So much for gratitude.

 Jubal

This was a great picture with Glenn Ford. I played a rancher who takes a shepherd in out of the cold and my wife falls in love with him. He ends up killing me in order to save his own life. Charlie Bronson was in the picture, along with Jack Elam and Rod Steiger, who had played *Marty* in a shorter television version before I did the movie. We had a great time. Rod didn't seem annoyed that I'd won an Oscar for a role he originated.

"I had *On the Waterfront*," he said. "I'm not greedy . . . and you were great."

I talked a little about Charlie Bronson before. This was about twenty years before he made the smash hit *Death Wish* and became the rage of Europe as well. He became a multimillionaire and was working like a son of a gun. His ability to "look," but not to say too much differentiated him from everyone else. My God, it paid off

You could always count on Charlie to give a good performance even if he had little or no dialogue. He'd mumble something or stumble or do something and always made it work. He never let his success go to his head. He never forgot his roots.

One day, about six years ago, I was working on a picture. A young man came over and said, "I want to introduce myself. You know my father."

I said, "Who's your father?"

He said, "Charlie Bronson."

I actually had tears in my eyes because he was such a nice young man, polite and respectful. I said to him, "How's your Dad?"

We'd been exchanging Christmas cards over the years, and I hadn't heard from him lately.

He said, "I'm sorry, but my dad is dying. He's got Alzheimer's disease."

That really took me by surprise and it hit me hard. But he'd had a good life, a great career, and in the end that isn't a bad thing.

 ## *The Catered Affair*

Bette Davis. Now there's an actress. She had already won two Best Actress Oscars by the time I met her in 1956. She was definitely Hollywood royalty, but didn't act like it.

Most of the time.

This one was written by Gore Vidal based on a play by Paddy Chayefsky—whose work had been good for me in the past—and directed by Richard Brooks, who went on to direct Burt Lancaster in his Oscar-winner *Elmer Gantry*. I didn't know it at the time, but Brooks ate and digested actors for breakfast. If things weren't working, he let you know it, and not gently.

I'll never forget the first morning I reported for the picture. It was the first time I'd met Bette Davis and Debbie Reynolds and I was a little bit in awe. We started rehearsing our scene on the set and things didn't seem to be working out.

Brooks said, "All right, work on the goddamn thing. I got to go behind camera and see what's happening there. I'll come back and we'll work it out."

So he went back to the camera and I said to Bette Davis, "Miss Davis, I think that I know what's wrong."

She said, "What is it?" She may have had a reputation for being tough, but she also knew how to play it soft and rally the troops.

I said, "It's a matter of timing and emphasis. Let's do the scene and I'll show you what I mean."

We did and it worked like a charm.

Brooks came back and said, "Awright, let's see if we can do this goddamn scene."

We ran through it and Brooks liked it.

Bette said, "You weren't watching, were you, Richard? Ernie here figured it out."

He took a look at me and said, without a hint of levity to suggest he might be kidding, "goddamn thinking actors."

We shot it, one take, and it was over.

We moved on to another set where I was going to be getting into bed with Bette. She was running her lines about giving her daughter a big wedding. Brooks got everybody around the bed and said, "All right, Mr. Borgnine. What do you have in mind for this scene?"

I blanched—what do I do now?—and looked at the bed.

I said, "Well, sir, I thought Miss Davis and I could do a variation of the wonderful story about a salesman who had been lugging these heavy suitcases all day long, just pulling and pushing and trying to sell things to the farmers. He finally got to this one farmer at night.

"He said, 'Please, I'm so tired. May I sleep in your barn tonight?'

"The farmer said, 'No. First you'll have dinner with us and then you'll bunk with my boy, who has a big bed.'"

By now the whole cast and crew is listening and watching.

I went on, "After dinner this man got up, excused himself, went right up and got into bed. Pretty soon the little boy came up and he got down by the side of the bed and bowed his head.

"The salesman opened one eye and thought, 'Gee, look at that. I haven't done anything like that since I was a young man. I'm going to get down on my side of the bed and pray.'

"The kid looked up at him and said, 'Mister, what you doing?'

"The man said, 'I'm doing the same thing you are, son.'

"The kid said, 'Gee, Mom's gonna be awful mad. The chamber pot's on this side!'"

Bette Davis let out a whoop. Richard Brooks never bothered me again.

Bette was "one of us," but she also had a sharp side. I was going over my lines while I was being photographed for some publicity shots by a well-known Sicilian photographer with one name. These were pictures studios give to newspapers and magazines to promote films that were in production—back in the days before stars were being photographed in unflattering positions by passersby with cell phones.

We were running a little late and as we were sitting there, a horse-shoe of beautiful pink roses was brought over to me by a stagehand. I read the card. It said, "Congratulations, Ernie. Now why don't you Italians go home?" It was signed "BD."

I thought it was the funniest thing in the world. I sought her out on the set and said, "Okay, let's go to work."

She replied, "Let's."

Working with her was one of the best experiences I've had on a film. She was a tiny thing, just five-foot-three, and always in motion. Smoking, shifting her shoulders this way and that, her eyes moving like little machines here and there missing nothing. You know, an actress in the 1930s didn't become as big as she was without having some steel in her backbone. But she never, ever used that muscle against her ensemble.

She ran into a career downturn during the late 1950s, until *What Ever Happened to Baby Jane?*—directed by my buddy Bob Aldrich—boosted her back to the top in 1962. I used to run into her over the years, when I lived up on Mulholland Drive and she lived alone in a small apartment building off the Sunset Strip. She was still feisty, still working into her late seventies, still a queen.

The Best Things in Life Are Free

It happens at least once to every actor, even the great ones like Marlon Brando.

They star, one time each, in a musical. My turn came in 1956.

Let me say, first of all, that this was my own choice and not a loan-out dictated by Hecht-Hill-Lancaster. We'd managed to settle that matter, which also enabled me to keep my whole fee for every picture I'd made. Hecht-Hill-Lancaster had showed me I could command $100,000 a film and that's what I continued to ask. I didn't want to go down but, at the time, I didn't want to price myself out of the market, either.

The Best Things in Life Are Free was a biography of the songwriting team Buddy De Sylva, Lew Brown, and Ray Henderson. I was asked to play Brown, with Gordon MacRae as De Sylva and Dan Dailey as Henderson. The main appeal for me was the chance to work with director Michael Curtiz. He may not be as well known as Alfred Hitchcock and John Ford, but he is, in my estimation, one of the most amazing directors who ever worked in film. *The Adventures of Robin Hood* with Errol Flynn. *Yankee Doodle Dandy. Casablanca.* Need I say more?

Actually, I do need to. He was a Hungarian. He had high heels. He always walked slanted forward. He was an eccentric. But boy, was he brilliant. The crew told me a story about when he was making the football picture *Jim Thorpe—All American* with Burt Lancaster. He came on the set, looked at the football field, and asked, "Where are all the men?" He was acting like this was *The Charge of the Light Brigade*, another of his classics.

They said, "That's all the men there are, Mr. Curtiz. Eleven on one side and eleven on the other."

He said, "That's not enough. Double it."

They said, "But sir—that's how American football is played!"

He said, "Double it, nobody will ever know the difference."

They doubled it and nobody ever knew the difference. He had men all over that field and it's the greatest football picture you ever saw.

One day we were doing a scene where Norman Brooks, playing Al Jolson, asked us to write him a song for a movie. He wanted to call the song "Sonny Boy." Now, Jolson was known for heart-wrenching *schmaltz* and the three songwriters made up the corniest song you could possibly imagine.

"Climb upon my knee, Sonny Boy, though you're only three, Sonny Boy . . ."

We actors knew it was corny, too. But let me tell you, when we saw the finished film and Brooks/Jolson finished singing it, everybody cried. Somebody in the audience said, "Jeez, this is the greatest song ever written."

It wasn't. It was still corn. But Jolson, and now Curtiz, made it work for the audience. And even though I was playing a songwriter in this musical, I was still required to throw a couple of punches in a scene where I confront some gangsters. Once a tough guy, always a tough guy.

After filming was completed, Curtiz presented me with a gold money clip. On it he wrote "To one of the finest actors I have ever worked with. Lovingly, Mike Curtiz." It was one of the most touching things that I had ever received, and from a director who, in my estimation, could do no wrong.

Just before he started working with us, Gordon MacRae had completed the film version of Rodgers and Hammerstein's *Carousel.* He invited us to come to the screening with him. This was a picture that was supposed to star Frank Sinatra, but Frank had walked off because every scene was being shot twice: once in CinemaScope and once for theaters that weren't equipped to show that widescreen process. He complained that he wasn't being paid for two movies.

I was very impressed with Gordon. He had a beautiful voice that came with no effort at all. He just let it all out. To think he died the way he did, cancer of the jaw in just his mid-sixties It was also a shame that drink got to him. He finally beat it and spent a lot of time counseling other alcoholics, but his problem also robbed us of a lot of the great work he might have done.

Fortunately, doing a musical didn't hurt my career as a serious actor—though, as you'll see in a while, getting up to sing a few years later nearly did me in.

Chapter 20

Talkin' Pictures, Part Two

 Three Brave Men (1956)

This one was a true story in which I played a man named Bernie Gold-smith, who was accused of being a communist simply because he thought it would be all right for blacks to live in a certain neighborhood with whites. Ray Milland was playing my lawyer, Joe. The third brave man was played by Frank Lovejoy. He played a captain who stood up for Goldsmith when he was dishonorably discharged from the navy.

I was doing a scene one day and asked my stand-in—someone who looks like you and stands there while they light the scene, so your makeup doesn't run and your energy doesn't flag—if he could find a record player and some 45s.

"Something spirited," I said. I wanted music we could play between shots because these scenes were so dramatic and down. We had to do something to lift ourselves up. He came back with a portable player and some Elvis records. We'd finish a scene and, *bam*, put on "Blue Suede Shoes" or "Hound Dog."

One day, Elvis's manager, Colonel Tom Parker, happened to be on the lot. He heard the music and walked over. He said, "I understand you like my boy Elvis."

I said, "Yes, I do, Colonel Parker."

He said, "I'd like to put you under contract."

I said, "I already have a contract, but thank you." I wasn't quite liberated from my old deal just yet.

He pulled out a contract; it must have been about six feet long.

He said, "Sign on the bottom line. I'll get you out of your contract."

Considering what he did for Elvis's career, maybe I should have gone with him, so help me. Either way, Colonel Parker was quite a character.

One day we were doing a scene in which my character had come home after being dismissed from the navy. I closed the door, pulled down the shades, and started to cry. Before we were finished I heard "Cut," then I heard somebody sobbing.

The director called me over and said, "Ernie, would you mind doing that scene over again?"

"Sure. Anything I can do to help?"

He said, "No, let's just do it again."

So I did it again and I got to the same place and I heard the sob again.

I stared into the lights and said, "What the hell is wrong?"

The director called me over and introduced me to this man, who turned out to be the real Bernie Goldsmith. Through tears, he said to me, "How did you know what I did when I came back to my house that day?"

It hadn't been written in the script, but I told him it was the most natural thing in the world to do. You shut yourself off from the world. You hate the world. You hate everything.

He said, "That's exactly the way I felt."

It really choked me up, and nothing like that has happened to me again. But I was lucky to experience it that once.

Thanks in part to our picture, Bernie Goldsmith was reinstated in the navy.

The Vikings (1958)

The Vikings was a box office smash and a lot of fun, unlike anything I'd ever played. Kirk Douglas, Tony Curtis, and Janet Leigh—at that time Mrs. Curtis, and also the mother of Jamie Lee—were the stars. I played the gruff, rough Ragnar, leader of the Viking clan. Our director was Richard Fleischer, a wonderful guy and an excellent director. He had recently directed Kirk in *20,000 Leagues Under the Sea*. You might say this one was *20,000 Leagues Over the Sea*. We spent a lot of time on the water!

We filmed on location and were feted generously all through Scandinavia. Everybody knew our pictures and everybody knew Tony, Janet, Kirk, and me. We shot much of the picture in Norway, in the Hardanger Fjord, onboard a full-size ship that had been constructed for the film. Kirk was producing the film, and had consulted several authorities on the specifics of the ship designs. Only hull fragments remained, and no one could agree on what they were really like. Kirk got fed up with these so-called experts. He personally went to a museum, measured a section of hull that had been dredged from some bog, and told his production people to make it "that big."

When we got to the fjord we were in civilian clothes. To row the Viking boats the production company had brought in oarsmen from all over Scandinavia. Some of these guys took one look at me and invited me to go for a little rowing practice.

I said, "Sure, let's go."

I knew exactly what was coming. These men wanted to test me. Well, I was hoping the joke would be on them. See, like most destroyers, my old ship the *Lamberton* had a whaleboat crew. I was the bow oar, which is a bitch, believe me. That was one of the hardest oars to row because you were almost rowing straight down. Lots of water to get through that way, but I got to be pretty adept at it. So we went out to the middle of the fjord, where I prayed to myself, "Whatever you do, don't catch a crab." In other words, don't miss a stroke because that screws everyone up and you're considered a jerk.

We started out nice and easy, pulling away from shore. Then we upped the stroke a little, then again. After a minute or so we were really pulling that boat. They kept this up for about five minutes before the crew chief said, "Toss the oars!" We took the fourteen foot oars out of the water and stood them up straight. They let out a cheer for Ragnar you could have heard all the way to Oslo. It was just like when we were shooting *Marty* in New York: after that, the locals made me one of their own.

Kirk was—and still is—a prince of a guy. He's a month older than me (funny since I was playing his father in the movie), so I've got to show respect . . . though he earned it anyway. As producer, he had the weight of the production on his shoulders. As star, he had to carry the film as well. He did both with unflappable grace. He's also a family man, and his young sons Michael and Eric were occasionally on the set, fighting with toy swords that had been made for them.

Janet Leigh was a sweetheart. Her main trouble when we were shooting *The Vikings* was sleeping at night because she had her infant, Kelly Curtis, with her. In fact, sleep was a problem for all of us, because it was sunshine all the time up there. They had to black out the curtains in all our rooms.

When the picture came out, I remember seeing a big sign for it in Times Square. It took up a whole block with a huge Viking boat and the four of us in it. It was just beautiful. That sign, which always advertised big movies, was there till about 1980 or so. Now, there's just giant TV screens and strobe lights. Folks used to say that huge billboard was overkill. I wonder what they'd think of Times Square today.

The Badlanders (1958)

This film did two things for me. It allowed me to work with another legend, Alan Ladd.

Alan and I took an immediate liking to each other. He was always on my tail because he knew that I was one of the guys who never used to go out at night. He kidded me, saying, "You were out there carousing last night and having a hell of a time on your own, weren't you?"

He knew I didn't do that because I was a married man. Working together we got to know each other pretty well, though I didn't know that he drank.

It was also on *The Badlanders* where I met the woman who would become my second wife. At the end of a particularly long and grueling day, the very first thing I heard the elegant and beautiful twenty-three-year-old Katy Jurado say was, "Who do I have to fuck to get off this picture?"

I was appalled! To hear a woman say that, then, left you a little bit chilled, you know?

But we got along fine and the next thing you know, Mike Connolly, the columnist, put two and two together. Actually, one and one. Because we had a love scene he thought we were an item. I complained that it wasn't true.

He said to me, "You two are a big deal."

I said, "Well, it's a lie."

He refused to print a retraction and I hated him from that day forward. That article was actually the proverbial last straw with Rhoda. Our marriage had been rocky for a long time at this point—sustaining a happy marriage is tough in Hollywood, where you're always surrounded by temptation. I was no exception.

When I finished on location in Mexico, I called Rhoda and told her I was coming home.

She said, icily, "You can't. My folks are visiting and there's no room for you."

"There's no room for me in my own bed and my own house?"

She said "Yeah." Seeing as how there was no rush, I took a train home with Alan Ladd. He wouldn't fly, and the ride gave me time to think. Now I knew it certain my marriage was over. I got a divorce. Rhoda not only got my brand-new Cadillac but also my old Cadillac as well. She got the house, everything. The only things I got to keep were my good looks.

Meanwhile, the press practically pushed Katy and I into a relationship. Gossip is what some people live for and some people live on. I'm not going to get on my soapbox about that, except to say that when you're on the receiving end it can be as personally destructive as a natural disaster. And there's nothing you can do to stop it.

As it happened, Katy and I ended up commiserating over that, and our lives. One thing led to another and then next thing you know we got married in 1959 and moved to Mexico. I don't think we were quite right for each other—Katy was beautiful, but a tiger. We separated and reconciled before finally separating for good in 1961. Our divorce became final in 1964—we took three years to fight over alimony.

As for Alan Ladd, I used to go up and visit him. I remember one day, about two years later, he said, "Ernie, I just can't understand people anymore."

I said, "What do you mean?"

He said, "I'm making this war picture, *All the Young Men*. There's a black man there that I can't understand and half the time I can't hear him. Is this the way they work today? Whispering?"

I said, "I guess it is."

The man turned out to be Sidney Poitier. That was his way of working and Alan just didn't get it. I've found myself pretty flexible over the years, maybe because I had so much diversity thrown at me right out of the gate, working with guys who did things the "Method" way like Monty Clift, actors who were singers who became actors like Frank, and actors who were acrobats who became actors like Burt— all on just one picture! I found it all pretty stimulating. Alan didn't.

Another time I was at his house when his little son David came in with a gift for his dad. It was a bottle opener.

It broke Alan's heart. I felt it and knew he felt it. The kid was being nice, unaware that his dad was struggling with drink. It was, in fact, what killed him when he was just fifty years old.

Alan never let on how terrible it made him feel about himself. After an awful pause he just said, "Thanks a lot son, thanks a lot."

A lot of people don't know that Alan almost made the Olympics swimming team in 1932. He was a superb athlete but he was really self-conscious about his size. He stood just under five-foot-five and he used to complain to me about being "a little man."

I would look at him with surprise and say, "You're little? For Chrissake, you're a giant among men!"

He didn't see it that way, and I think that was one of the reasons he drank. He stayed alone a lot. I remember once having to force him to come to a party at my house. We had Bob Mitchum, Rita Hayworth, a whole bunch of people who loved and respected him. He came and had a great time, but it was one of the few times I saw him actually having fun.

I was so very happy for his son, Alan Ladd, Jr., who did really well as the head of Twentieth Century-Fox, where he green-lighted the first *Star Wars* in 1977, and *Alien*, among many other box office hits. Alan would have been very proud of him. Alan also would've gotten a kick out of the later success of another friend of his who used to hang around. He didn't have much money, and was grateful for a meal. He would help Alan with his lines, do odd jobs—a fellow named Aaron Spelling, who eventually became one of the most successful TV producers and richest men in Hollywood.

 Torpedo Run (1958)

I had an interesting first day on this picture.

Glenn Ford was the star and, God bless him, from the very first day he wanted to show a little bit of his authority. He made the director, Joseph Pevney—who went on to have a huge career in TV—kind of take a backseat to show that he was the star.

We were doing a scene with a periscope going up and Glenn taking a look before sending it down again. After the first take Glenn said, "No, I don't like it."

The crew pulled it up again and pulled it down again.

"No, I don't like it."

We did that a couple of times. Suddenly Glenn turned to me and said, "What did you think of it?"

I said, "I liked the first one."

He blew up. Lunch was called and the producer came down to the set and said, "What's wrong here? Who wants to go first?"

Glenn said, "I will." He started out blaspheming everyone and everything, and then said, "If this things fails, I get the blame. I just want things to be right."

The producer listened, then said, "Okay, fine. Anybody else?"

Nobody said a word. Not even the director. Well, Glenn *was* the star. And what he said was true, even if he made his point a little aggressively.

The producer said, "All right, then," and we went back to work. From then on Glenn was cooperative, one of the guys, and everyone was very alert to his feelings.

I went up to see Glenn years later in the hospital, not long before his death. The very first thing out of his mouth when he saw me, was, "It was my fault, I'm sorry. I'm terribly sorry."

He had remembered after all that time.

They don't make stars like that anymore!

Chapter 21

Talkin' Pictures, Part Three: Abroad

 Man on a String (1960)

New decade, old director.

In 1960 I did a film based on the true exploits of a double agent. He was originally an agent for the Soviet Union until the United States found out about him. They said, "You're going to turn around and be an agent for us," and he did. I played the spy, Boris Mitrov, and dear Kerwin Mathews was my American contact. We shot the picture in Berlin.

When we started, André De Toth, the director, told us to be very careful because people were being taken off the streets and whisked away into East Germany, where they were never heard from again. He took me into East Berlin before the wall went up.

One day I was doing a scene with a guy on Berlin's old Embassy Row, where my character asked him, "Can't we just get out for a minute and have a smoke?"

He said, "Okay."

So we got out of the car and since I was handcuffed, I asked him for a cigarette.

He gave me a cigarette and I was able to work my lighter, which was actually a small-caliber gun. A pellet went into his neck, he dropped, and I started to run. Across the street were about ten Russian soldiers. Watching the scene, they wondered what the hell was going on. As I started to run, one of them pointed his gun. I stopped and said, "Nein, nein, schauspieler, schauspieler," which meant "actor" in German. Luckily they understood. It was *Vera Cruz* all over again! I'm fortunate to have survived my chosen profession.

In the same picture, we had an airplane that was supposed to be from Russia. It had CCCP on the side and all that. Well, they rolled this phony Russian plane out of the hangar. Now, alongside this airport was a row of trees and in those trees the Russians had built supposedly secret observation posts so they could watch the comings and goings of the British personnel who ran the field, and could see into the rooms where the British put information on blackboards. Naturally, they put up a lot of false information for the Russians to copy.

Well, out came this airplane. I swear to God you could actually see the trees trembling like crazy because everybody was going nuts. I could almost hear them saying, "My God, did we take over? What's happened?"

We were supposed to taxi and take off, but suddenly the British commander came running over to De Toth.

"Excuse me a minute, sir, would you look up there?" the officer said, pointing.

De Toth looked up, and so did I. A Russian fighter plane was circling.

The commander said, "They apparently think we've stolen one of their aircraft and are taking it somewhere for study. Your plane wouldn't get fifteen feet off the ground before it would be dead meat."

De Toth changed his plans.

Kerwin was just a honey of a guy. Some of you may know him for his three big fantasy films, *The 7th Voyage of Sinbad*, *The Three Worlds of Gulliver*, and *Jack the Giant Killer*. He liked acting but never got the breaks that you need to become a star. Not long thereafter he retired and opened a flower shop in San Francisco. He died a few years back.

Soon after we shot our picture the Russians put up their wall. When I returned to Berlin some years later, I climbed a ladder to look over. It was a horrible thing. They had put rollers along the edge so that would-be escapees from East Berlin couldn't get a grip on the edge They added ball bearings on top in case someone did get on top, and past the barbwire there. The minute you hit the ball bearings you'd make a racket. If you didn't get shot, you'd slip and fall back.

Seeing that, I swore to myself I'd never complain about the hardships of my chosen profession. And if I haven't said it before now, let me state for the record: God bless America.

Pay or Die (1960)

This was another true story, about Giuseppe Petrosino, who had been a lieutenant in the New York police force. He had done such a good job cleaning up the Mafia in New York that Teddy Roosevelt and the King of Italy, Victor Emmanuel, thought that they'd like him to take on the Mafia in Palermo.

It's funny how little things can undo you. Here was this guy who was so careful while he was undercover. He wore a disguise and the gangsters didn't know what he looked like. Well, evidently, he was heading for the post office box to send off a message to the United States and these Mafioso knew that he was in town. They carried shotguns and went around yelling "Petrosino, Petrosino."

Without thinking, he said, "yes," and they shot him full of holes on the Piazza Marina in March of 1909.

The highlight of *Pay or Die*—which were the words the Italian Black Hand (the forerunner of the Mafia at the turn of the twentieth century in America) would print on a piece of paper and hand to their extortion victims—was when I get pushed in front of a subway train barreling into the station. People still ask me about that scene today.

Pay or Die was one of the great pre-*Godfather* Mafia movies.

 ## Go Naked in the World (1961)

This melodrama starred Tony Franciosa and Gina Lollobrigida. Tony was all right, but we hated Gina. She was difficult to work with. It got to a point where, one time, Tony ran her right into a post at the bottom of the stairs. I mean, he ran her right into it. *Kaboom!*

That poor director, Ranald MacDougall. He wanted to make a shot of her walking on the beach as the sun was going down. Everyone kept saying to her, "Come on, come on, the sun is setting." But she said, "I have to paint my toenails first." Of course, they lost the shot. And they never would have seen her toes. I guess she needed that to get in character or something.

Gina didn't know that I could speak Italian. Her husband was telling her in Italian, "You have to give it more, this guy's got too much balls for you." But as she cranked it up, so did I. I knew exactly what she was doing.

I never said a word. Then one night after work, I said to her in perfect Italian, *"Senora, di buona notte, era il mio piacere funzionare con voi!"*—"Good night, senora, it was my pleasure to work with you."

She turned white down to her painted toes.

 ## Barabbas (1961)

I hadn't worn a toga in a while. I guess producer Dino De Laurentiis thought the world needed another dose of that when he phoned and asked me to appear in his biblical epic starring Tony Quinn as the criminal who was freed when Jesus was sent to the cross.

There wasn't much of a part for me. They already had Jack Palance as the bad-boy gladiator and Arthur Kennedy as Pontius Pilate. My then-wife Katy Jurado had been cast, and my old buddy Richard Fleischer was directing. Those were all good reasons to do the picture. I told Dino I'd consider it.

He said, "We'll give you $25,000."

That was damn good for what amounted to three-quarters of an hour's work. I could tell Dino really wanted me, and I decided to push it. I happened to be thumbing through a magazine that had pictures of Ferraris.

Man, I thought, *that's a good-looking car.*

I said, "I'll do it for $25,000 and a Ferrari."

I could hear Dino gulp over the phone two or three times. But, you know, it meant a lot to pictures in those days to have an all-star cast looking out from those big billboards like the one in Times Square. I was betting he'd bite. And he did.

He said, "Okay, and a Ferrari."

My American agent said to me later, "Jesus Christ, I think I'm going to have you as *my* agent!" Yeah, well—you know what I think of agents.

Barabbas came out at the tail end of the biblical cycle, after *Ben-Hur* and *King of Kings* had covered that territory in big, hugely popular style. There was no room for an epic but reverent, relatively subdued film about this tortured man who finally discovered Christianity. The movie was a box-office disappointment. I felt bad for Tony, who did some great work, and particularly for Katy, since a hit would have bumped her up a few notches in terms of popularity.

That's show business. Sometimes, even God can't help you.

After *Barabbas* I stayed in Rome to do another Italian-language picture starring Vittorio Gassman, the Italian actor who was married to Shelley Winters. It was called *I Briganti Italiani* (*The Italian Brigands* was the American title).

Life imitates art—Katy played my wife in the picture. Our marriage was starting to disintegrate around this time. The pressures of trying to sustain a marriage when both of us were off working were taking their toll.

My most vivid memory, though, had nothing to do with us. One day I was doing this big scene, giving this impassioned speech to a bunch of people under a tree. Suddenly, I stopped.

The director, a pleasant man named Mario Camerini, said, "Why did you stop?"

I said, "When he gets through picking his nose, I'll go ahead."

So help me Christ, Gassman was actually picking his nose on camera!

Chapter 22

At Sea Again: McHale's Navy Is Launched

One thing I hate is downtime. I get fidgety and cranky when I'm not working. It goes against that work ethic my parents instilled in me.

During the ten-year period when I was making pictures, there were lulls—and I hated them. Whenever I had a little free time, and whenever there was a good project, I'd return to TV. From 1951 to 1961 I did a bunch of things, mostly anthology shows, which have since gone the way of the dinosaur—*The Ford Television Theatre, Fireside Theatre, The O. Henry Playhouse, Schlitz Playhouse of Stars*, and *The Zane Grey Theater*. The ones that spelled theater "theatre" were a little snootier. Unlike a lot of actors, I had no compunction about jumping from one medium to the other. I didn't feel television was a comedown. Hell, more people saw me on one of those shows in a single night than saw any one of my movies during its entire run.

So in late 1961 when Universal asked me if I'd do an hour drama, *Seven Against the Sea*, I said, "Sure." It was a pilot for a possible series—meaning that if it was good it would be picked up for a year's worth of episodes. There was going to be an ensemble cast—well, seven—which meant that if it became a weekly show and I had to go off and make a movie, I could. If the pilot was bad, they'd air it once in the small hours of the night just to recoup some of the costs. Unfortunately, it didn't turn out too well. It was telecast on April 3, 1962, on *Alcoa Premiere*, and that was that.

Jennings Lang, a former agent and now a producer at Universal, saw it and had an idea. Now, not all of Jennings's ideas were good. For instance, there was the time in 1951 when he supposedly had an affair with actress Joan Bennett. Joan's husband, producer Walter Wanger, found out about it and shot Jennings right in the crotch.

But this idea happened to be good. Lang said to the suits at Universal, "Why don't we turn this thing around? We've got the boat, we've got the lake at the studio. Why don't we take this same basic concept, turn it around, and make it a comedy?"

That's how *McHale's Navy* was born. I played the Commander of a PT Boat in the South Pacific during World War II.

People assume that because I was in the navy during World War II, the show must've been my idea. I wish it was. I'd be making a lot more trips to the bank. See, I don't get any royalties—back then, the rules said they stopped after seven reruns—but the creators still do. I was just a working stiff.

Edd Henry, a bigwig at Universal, was the one who called me and made the offer for me to star.

At first, I was kind of cool to the idea. Not that it was a *bad* idea. Phil Silvers had done okay for himself playing *Sgt. Bilko* on TV. *McHale's Navy* was in many ways a knockoff of *Bilko*, which had been a huge hit. But I had other considerations.

I said, "You know, a commitment like that would really limit the amount of time I have to make movies."

He said, "True. But you'd make more money if the show is a hit and there are toys with your face on them. Then you'd be even more valuable to a movie producer."

He had a point. I told him I'd think about it

As I said, I hate being idle—which I happened to be, at the moment. Living in Mexico with Katy had kept me off the Hollywood radar, so we had moved back to Los Angeles. She was working on TV in a lot of westerns and I was waiting for the phone to ring. I hadn't made a picture since returning from Italy, almost a year. I should add that after a distinguished film career of nearly twenty years, Katy wasn't happy to be doing TV. She *did* see it as a step backward. With her unhappy and me unemployed, getting out of the house seemed like a good idea. Especially since we were living on Mulholland Drive and Universal was a short hop down the hill.

The next morning, as the good Lord would have it, a kid came to the door selling chocolate bars from a school out in the San Fernando Valley.

As I was digging through my pocket for money, the kid said, "Mister, your face looks awfully familiar. What's your name?"

I kidded him and said, "My name is James Arness."

The kid frowned. "Naw, he does *Gunsmoke.*"

I said, "You got me. I'm really Richard Boone."

He said, "He does *Have Gun Will Travel.*"

I thought, *Son of a gun, this kid knows them all, doesn't he?*

I told him, "My name is Ernest Borgnine."

That got no response. Absolutely nothing!

He said, "I know I've seen you somewhere."

"I won an Academy Award for *Marty,*" I told him.

"Anything else?" he asked.

I said, "Yeah—buncha things you may have seen. Probably on TV."

I paid for the chocolate bars, put them on the table, went to the telephone, picked it up.

"Edd," I said, "that part still open?"

He said, "Yeah."

I said, "Good. I'll do it."

He said, "What changed your mind?"

I said, "Richard Boone," and let it go at that.

The next year, after the first season of *McHale's Navy*—which was a smash beyond all our expectations—I found myself up in Oregon somewhere looking for a place to stay for the night. Katy and I had separated and I was looking for a place to hide from her—and her divorce lawyers. I poked my head into this cabin and the guy looked at me and said, "McHale! What are you doing here?"

Thank God for that kid and his chocolate bars.

I have to admit, I had a lot of fun that first season. I felt really kind of decadent getting up at a reasonable hour each day, driving three miles to the lot, spending my free time in a real dressing room with a real telephone to conduct business, shooting till dinnertime, then going home. It sure beat getting up before dawn to drive to Lonesome Pine, freezing my ass off, and waiting around to say a line or two and get punched.

Plus, there was something in the air at the time. TV was becoming big business. Up till now, a lot of shows had been made by independent producers who had been making low-budget movies in the 1940s and 1950s and just moved their crews and talent into low-budget TV. Universal was one of the first studios to see that there was a fortune to be made in this new medium, and the studio was just starting to make that transition.

By the time *McHale* ended its run, we'd be doing the episodes in color. Color TV really caused the medium to grow. In fact, it was during this time that Universal built the infamous "black tower" on the back lot. That's the office building on Lankershim Boulevard—since dwarfed by an even larger black tower. The scuttlebutt on the lot was that the accountants were moving in and taking over, and that proved to be the case. The actors didn't feel it, but the producers did. They could no longer call someone like a Louis B. Mayer or a Darryl F. Zanuck or a Walt Disney and say, "Chief, I need another two weeks and an extra million bucks to finish this picture" and get a yea or nay that day. Now it had to go to a committee and, more often than not, you were turned down.

Also, during our four years on the air, Universal started conducting studio tours. The back lot was always abuzz with activity and the smiling faces of fans as the trams came through. Back then, the tour actually visited working sets like ours. In fact, the studio hired one of my costars, Bob Hastings, to meet and greet the fans. It was a real thrill for them, and for him. We used to pop out of the bushes with spears in our hands and scare the tourists. That was fun for us, till one day a big old fat lady fell out of the tram. The front office said, "No more attacking the tourists!"

I have to admit, one thing I never expected was the joy of working day after day with a brilliant ensemble. Tim Conway is a comic genius and in no small way one of the reasons *McHale's Navy* was so successful. He was always ad-libbing and coming up with comic bits that kept the show fresh and the cast on our toes. You had to be sharp to act with him. Gavin MacLeod is also a great talent who went on to great fame on *The Mary Tyler Moore Show*, where he was a standout, and later as the captain of *The Love Boat*. Joe Flynn, a lovely guy and TV veteran, brought a lot to the show as well. I was shocked when he died a few years after we went off the air, drowning when he suffered a heart attack while swimming. He was just forty-nine. Then there was Bob Hastings, whose brother Don I mentioned earlier, having worked with him in New York in the fifties. Bob also popped up in a film I did, *The Poseidon Adventure*, where he played the emcee counting down the new year as a big wave raced toward the ship.

We had a great time on *McHale's Navy*. We got to know each other and the routine so well, in fact, that one time we could have finished an episode in a day and a half instead of three days. I said, "No, let's come back and finish tomorrow. Otherwise, Universal will have us shooting each show in a day and a quarter!"

The people behind the camera loved working on our show because we had so many laughs. Crews would fight to be assigned to us. Let me tell you, that never happened on any feature film I ever worked on before or since!

There's a tradition, after the first season, for the stars to buy something for the cast and crew. So I got everyone personalized red, white, and blue sweaters with McHALE'S NAVY written on the back. Everybody went nuts and started wearing them around the studio. One day, Lew Wasserman, the head of the studio, came up and said, "All right, where's mine?" So I had to run around like crazy and try to get one, then had one of the wardrobe gals sew "Lew" on it. I never saw the son of a gun wear it, but he had one.

The only unpleasant memory of the show was when our producer, Edward Montagne, would come down to see the dailies, the raw footage shot the day before. He got the job because he'd been a supervising producer on the *Bilko* show. For the first part of the first season, I'd ask Ed what he thought. He'd grumble and not really answer. One of the writers, a sweetheart named Si Rose, would watch the same dailies and when I asked him he'd always say, "Great—you guys are doing a hell of a job." That was important, because we hadn't gone on the air yet and had no idea how people would react. All actors need feedback, and producers should be willing to give it. Usually, they do. In fact, it's tough to keep them from interfering.

So one day I approached this producer. I said, "Why don't you come down to the set once in a while and tell the guys they're doing a good job? It'd mean a lot to 'em and they do work hard."

He looked at me like he'd swallowed a bug. "I don't kiss anybody's ass," he said.

I said, "Hey, I'm not asking you to kiss any ass. Just pat 'em on the back a little."

He said, "Insecure actors. Jesus," and walked away.

Well, I grabbed him to turn him back around and we really got into it. I ripped his shirt and he ripped mine. We almost came to blows. Luckily we didn't. This producer directed us a few times, at the very beginning. It was a disaster, because this guy didn't know how to direct his way out of a toilet. We'd finally work it out on our own, when he was busy doing something else, and he'd say "Okay, let's do it that way." As if he'd thought of it!

McHale's Navy ran four seasons. It could have gone on a lot longer, but the producer insisted that we move the crew of PT 73 from the fictional Pacific island of Taratupa to Italy in order to give us fresh storylines. You know, that kind of move is always a disaster, like marrying two characters like Jeannie and Col. Nelson or Lois and Clark. Introduce new characters, send 'em to Italy or Hawaii or wherever for a two-parter, but don't fix what ain't broken! Fans didn't like the new approach and we were canceled a lot sooner than we should have been. Still, we made 148 episodes and had a great time with every one of them. As I write this, early in 2008, I still get letters from people who grew up with the show and—believe it or not—forty years later Tim Conway and I still work together, doing voices on the kids' Saturday cartoon show, *SpongeBob SquarePants!* I bitch from time to time, but this *can* be a great business. How many people do you know who are still working with old colleagues after so many years?

It's kind of funny, though. I'm still working with Tim after four decades. But when it comes to women . . .

Chapter 23

Everything's Coming Up Roses—Not

There's no business like show business.

You've all heard that famous song lyric, right? As I just said about *McHale's Navy*, it's been pretty great for me. Sadly, the marriage business took me a lot longer to get right.

I met Ethel Merman in the spring of 1964, after the show's second season had wrapped. I was at a party where everybody was begging some woman to get up and sing. I had heard of her, of course, from her Broadway triumphs *Annie Get Your Gun* and *Gypsy*. But I hadn't seen them and I didn't recognize her.

I was standing by the piano listening. She started singing and my eyes lit up. I said, "My God, she's got a voice! It's incredible!" She was singing Cole Porter and other standards.

When she was finished, we happened to end up standing side by side at the bar. She looked over and said, "You like that?"

I said, "I loved it. That was marvelous!"

She asked, "Who are you?"

"My name is Ernest Borgnine."

"Oh, yes," she said. "You're that funny guy on *McHale's Navy*."

"That's right."

I was a little miffed that she hadn't recognized me from *Marty*, but then, I hadn't recognized her, either.

We talked for hours and the first thing you know the twice-divorced Ethel Agnes Zimmermann and I were an item. It was wonderful—at first. She lived in New York and I lived in L.A. She had to return east but we were always on the phone to each other.

It was ridiculous. We decided she'd move to Los Angeles and we'd get married. Ethel had recently had a hit with her costarring role in the comedy *It's a Mad Mad Mad Mad World*, and since nothing was brewing on the stage, she decided to try and build on that.

We had a big wedding in my backyard in Beverly Hills. It was quite beautiful and everybody had a great time. Lovebirds were released from cages and flew all over the place. Everyone was enthralled.

Biggest mistake of my life. Maybe I thought I was marrying Rosemary Clooney, who knows?

For our honeymoon, we decided to go Hawaii, Japan, and Hong Kong. It was June and I didn't have to be back for the third season of *McHale's Navy* for another six weeks. So off we went to Hawaii.

It was a disaster.

Everybody in Hawaii seemed to know me. It was, "Hey, Mr. Borgnine, how are you?" and "Ernie, how are you?"

Nobody said a thing about my wife, and I was always saying, "This is the great Ethel Merman."

Only a few people seemed to care. It was embarrassing for me and humiliating for her.

When we got to Kyoto, Japan, the same thing happened. She became more and more distant as the trip went on. By the time we got to Hong Kong she was hardly speaking to me—just because I was more famous than her. I tried to understand. As I've said, it's tough for women in this business. When they're strong, when they stand up for themselves, they're called "bitches." It isn't right, but that's the way it was back then . . . and today, too, though a little less so. Ethel wasn't a bitch, but she was just naturally competitive in a very competitive business. She reacted strongly and emotionally to what she suddenly viewed as a contest between her and me.

In Hong Kong, an unfortunate thing happened. I caught the *turista* real bad. She got a little dose of it, but, man, I was really out. An agent from Cooks Tour, who had arranged our trip, came to see me. Ethel was lying in the big bed all by herself. I was in the sitting room next door, flopped across a couch, sicker than a dog. He came in and said, "Mr. Borgnine, you've got to get packed. You're due on the plane back to Hawaii."

I looked up at him and said, "I don't think I can make it."

He said, "I'll help you, but you've got to go. This room is booked."

He knocked on Ethel's door and went in. She said she was well enough to leave and he started to help her pack. Then he saw this vial of medicine she had for her sickness.

"Would you like to give some to your husband?" he asked. "He's really badly off."

She said, "Why should I? It belongs to me."

I heard that. It was enough to get me off the couch and out of Hong Kong. That pretty much did it as far as I was concerned.

When we got to Hawaii, Ethel ran right to a telephone to tell her mother and dad how badly I treated her. I hadn't done anything to her. I hadn't touched her. When we got home, we were invited to her lawyer's home for dinner. She was still mad at me, now I was mad at her, and we weren't talking at all. It was stupid, in a way, because I hadn't done anything. But there we were.

While we were eating she started telling the story of how I had mistreated her by hogging the limelight wherever we went. That was it. I looked at this woman and just shook my head. Then I got up and walked out.

The next morning she said, "What do you mean by leaving?"

"Madam," I said, "as far as I'm concerned, this marriage is over. You call your people and I'll get my people and we'll come to a settlement."

Well, she was furious. *Furious!* It was so over the top it was like she was playing a scene.

"How dare you?" she screamed. "What do you mean? You can't do this."

I said, "What do you mean I can't? You want to live like this for the rest of your life?"

She said, "No! So just stop being a publicity hound!"

That was it. I went to work and lived in my dressing room at the studio.

One day on the set, her lawyer showed up—a nice man, actually. He said, "She'd like to have you come back to her."

I said, "Well, that's very nice. But would you like to hear exactly what happened while we were away?"

He said, "Okay."

So we had lunch together in a quiet corner at the commissary and I told him exactly what happened from the time we got married until the day we returned from the wedding trip. When I was finished, he looked at me and I looked at him.

I asked, "Would *you* go back?"

He smiled. "No."

So Ethel packed up all her things and shipped them home and I paid for it. She went back to her apartment in New York and that was the end of that.

Almost.

Cut to thirty years later. I was doing a show called *Ernest Borgnine on the Bus* with my son Cris. It was a fun documentary where we drove across America, talking to people and telling stories. A buddy of mine, Hugo Hansen, had come along and we ended up in Iowa on the 4th of July. It was a nice, clear day after several days of rain.

After the 4th of July celebration, Hugo and I started walking around this little town. We walked into a storefront that had been turned into a kind of makeshift museum. There were some old things there including World War II uniforms and a lot of books.

Hugo picked up a book and said, "Hey, look at this. It's written by Ethel Merman."

I had heard that she had written a memoir, but I had never seen it. Ethel had been dead for about twelve, thirteen years at the time and I was in a forgiving mood.

I said, "Let's open it and see what it says."

There was a chapter heading that read "Ernest Borgnine." It was a blank page. That was it!

I said, "At least she didn't say anything bad about me."

Poor gal. Ethel was a very, very great talent and a wonderful person . . . when she wasn't married. What happened to us is a lesson in the downside of fame, which is one reason never to pursue it as a goal in itself. If it comes, okay, you deal with it. If it doesn't, then—like the kid who sold me chocolates that time—you roll with it. Besides, being famous isn't all it's cracked up to be. Yeah, you never have to wait for a table at a crowded restaurant. But you can't take your kids to Disneyland, either. It's a wash.

In the end, life and love and career are all hard enough without adding fame into the mix!

Chapter 24

The Fourth Estate

This might be a good time to pause and discuss gossip, because Ethel and I generated a bunch of it when we split.

You may find this difficult to believe, but a lot—not everything, mind you, but a lot—of what's written about celebrities is bull. You say, "So why don't you sue?" Well, there are two reasons. First, it's expensive. Lawyers charge you a grand just to say "hello." Second, it's a grueling process. You have to get deposed by the opposing side, which can take days. They ask you all kinds of personal questions that become part of the public record. Very often, people sue the tabloids, then end up dropping the case after a few weeks. They make their big public show, protest that the stories aren't true, and then everything goes away, booted aside by the next big story.

So many of the women I worked with, in particular, have gotten a bum rap. It's not true, for example, that Joan Crawford and Bette Davis were enemies. I worked with them both. They had days when they were up and days when they were a little down. They were competing for the same roles. And for women of a certain age, those parts are pretty rare. Of course they were rivals. But enemies? They were both part of the Hollywood social circles and were photographed a lot and—

well, newspaper people have to write something to go with a picture. Kate Hepburn didn't go out a lot and no one ever wrote that she hated, I don't know, Vivien Leigh or Barbara Stanwyck.

But if Joan and Bette showed up at the same dinner or ceremony, and did a kind of fake snarl for the press, they were written up as having a feud. If they were adversaries in a film, like *What Ever Happened to Baby Jane?* then people assumed they were battling in real life (an idea sometimes given a little push by overeager studio publicists looking for press). You want to know what I remember most about Bette Davis? Her big, explosive laugh, which was really something, and the fact that she never went anywhere unless she was "put together," as she described it. If she hated anything, it was the idea that stars would ever go out looking like slobs. But there's a difference between that and hating the star who does it!

Hey, I'm not saying everyone gets along. I've told you several times when that wasn't the case. But most of the time, we do. We're all pulling for the same thing, for a picture or TV show to be a success. Some people handle that pressure a little less adroitly than others. Usually, though, that doesn't last. If it does—or if there's a problem like pills or booze—they get the heave-ho by the front office.

Most of us are homebodies, actually. After a long day of shooting, you have to memorize lines, go to sleep, wake up, and do it all over again. There are costume fittings and traveling to locations and rehearsals. Who has time to tear another actor a new one? And when I get through with a picture there's nothing I want more than to just sit around my house and enjoy it. I love being at home, especially when there's family around.

But the gossips won't let you do that. They think, "We've got to sell some more papers." So they find a photo where you look a little tired and they say you're drunk. They have you leaning over to kiss someone and now you're an item. If it happens to be a guy, you're gay. They find some smut to say about you and the first thing you know people come up and say, "Is it true that you did so and so?"

Some people handle it better than others. Liz Taylor, for example. All those romances, all those illnesses—the press was after her in a way that makes Paris Hilton look like a hermit. But she stayed above it, all class, true Hollywood royalty. But then you have someone like poor Natalie Wood. She was a star since she was a little kid in *Miracle on 34th Street*. She hung out with Elvis, James Dean, Warren Beatty, with the press in tow the entire time. But she was basically just this quiet girl who wanted to have a life. When she couldn't have it, she drank. She retired for a while. In the end, she never did manage to get her feet under her and was dead at the age of forty-three. Shirley MacLaine's got spunk. She made it on Broadway, she made it in film, and she became a best-selling author writing about past lives and stuff that a lot of people think is nuts. She didn't care. She had what I talked about before—steel in her backbone.

You need talent or good looks or a great voice or some other distinctive angle or all of the above to break into this business. You need stamina to stay in it . . . and a real thick skin. Mary Tyler Moore once said something that was dead-on. She said, "Men who want to get ahead are called 'ambitious.' Women who want that are called things that are a lot less flattering."

She was right. That happens a little in the casting offices, but it happens a whole lot more in the press. And it's wrong.

Hopefully, where my life is concerned, this book will set the record straight. I wasn't always an angel, but then who is?

Chapter 25

Back to the Big Screen

Contrary to popular wisdom, being on TV didn't prevent me from going back to movies. See, Hollywood has this idea that if audiences can see you for free at home, they won't pay to see you in the movies. That didn't stop Bruce Willis or John Travolta from making the jump, but it's still "common wisdom" out here.

While I was still doing *McHale's Navy* I shot *The Flight of the Phoenix* outside of Yuma, Arizona. Bob Aldrich directed and Jimmy Stewart starred. It was a taut picture about a bunch of guys trying to get out of the desert after a plane crash. It was a clever movie, not only in terms of plot but also character: every crewmember personified the attributes of a nation that had been involved in World War II.

Jimmy Stewart was just wonderful. Like all the old pros—Spencer Tracy, James Cagney, Gary Cooper—he knew his lines and even when he wasn't on camera, he was there to act with you. A lot of stars just go to their trailer and let a script girl read the lines. Not him. He was always hanging around; you couldn't go too far because it was the middle of the desert, but I've heard he did that on every movie he made. God, I envied him, though: he made it look so easy. I know it wasn't. He studied his lines and he rehearsed with the rest of us. But when it came out, it was as though he were saying the lines for the first time.

It was great to be working with Bob Aldrich again. However, something happened between us that hadn't happened before or since. I was doing a scene with Peter Finch, whose character was about to set out across the desert. My character wanted to go with him. He said I was needed at the wreck and I went a little nuts, starting to fight everyone. Finally, they held me and I settled down.

When we finished the scene, I heard a kind of a strangled cry: "Cut!" I looked over at Bob and he was crying like a baby. The scene had really affected him.

He said, "Would you mind trying it again?"

I said, "No, not at all. Is there anything you want me to do?"

He said, "No. It was just so goddamn good I have to see it again."

So we did it over and he cried again. It was amazing.

I have to say, I don't get it when men are bashful about showing emotion. I've had it happen many times in my life, where I'll be talking about someone who did something kind or brave, or someone who is no longer with us, or who did some incredible piece of work. I'll get choked up and start to weep. Often, I have to stop what I'm saying because everybody else gets all choked up too, because they're right there with me.

I believe in showing emotions, showing that you have a heart. I cried doing that scene in the movie because that's how I felt. When you can make your audience—which includes your director—feel it, too, you're doing what an actor is supposed to do.

What a person should do.

 ## The Dirty Dozen (1967)

Some of the most fun I've had on movie sets was with my buddy Lee Marvin. When it was Lee *and* Bob Aldrich, with Charlie Bronson thrown in for good measure, it was pure heaven.

Need I say it? *The Dirty Dozen* was pure heaven—though not at first.

I was on an airplane coming back from New York, where I'd been doing some promotional things for *McHale's Navy*. My agent at the time, Ronnie Lief, had come with me.

We were going over some business when Ronnie said, "MGM is going to be shooting a picture called *The Dirty Dozen* over in England and I'm going to see if I can get you on it."

I said, "That's great, who's directing?"

He said, "Bob Aldrich."

Ronnie didn't have to do any arm-twisting to get me into the picture. Luckily, the shoot was scheduled during a *McHale's Navy* hiatus. What a project that was. Lee played an army major who had to assemble a team of cons, real misfits, for a suicide mission during World War II. It turned out to be my most successful film to date. If anyone needed proof that audiences could accept me as something other than Quinton McHale, *The Dirty Dozen* was it.

I'd married Donna Rancourt in 1965. In the summer of 1966, I took her and our two young kids, Sharon and Cris, with me to England.

I'd never advise anyone to travel that way, carrying your family with you when you've got to work. I had costume fittings and lines to learn and rehearsals, starting at once, but I also had to find an apartment for them, close to stores and museums and theaters. I was nearly burned out before we started!

Unlike the States, you're allowed to drink on movie sets in England. Because of that, I saw a side of Lee Marvin I'd never seen. Lee was drinking up pretty good from noon till night. He said he was still celebrating from having won his Best Actor Oscar as the drunk gunfighter in *Cat Ballou*. I don't know. That had happened about three or four months before. I wondered if he was taking that part too close to heart!

He and I were standing near a wall talking when a crew member went by from our group and said, "I wonder what two Academy Award winners have to say to each other?"

Without missing a beat, Lee looked up and said, "You'll never know," and went right on talking.

I was flabbergasted. I'd never seen Lee cut someone down like that. The poor guy just died right on the spot.

It got worse.

We were rehearsing one day and we got through with my stuff so Aldrich called to have Jim Brown brought onto the set.

Lee said, "Yeah, bring in the nigger."

Well, there was a long silence and then Aldrich said to Lee, "Would you mind stepping into my office for a moment?"

Lee was feeling pretty good and he said, "Sure."

The two of them went to the small production office in the corner of the soundstage. They came out about ten minutes later. Lee was absolutely sober from that minute forth. Never a demeaning word or anything on his breath when he was working. I don't know if Jim ever heard about what Lee said. Probably not. The former football star was not someone you wanted to cross.

After Bob Aldrich screened the movie for the execs at MGM, he was told that he could win the Oscar for Best Director for the film if he cut out the scene of Jim Brown dropping hand grenades into the bomb shelter. The scene had a lot of the suits uneasy—it *is* pretty brutal and they were afraid the critics would crucify him. Aldrich, God bless him, never cared much what the critics had to say. The scene stayed in the picture.

Things went fine after that and we all had a ball. It shows in the finished film. Even though most of the cast ends up under a pile of rocks, audiences remember the movie fondly and it's one they always want to talk to me about, a real classic.

You're lucky if you get one of those in your career, a classic. I've had several. Like I said, I'm a lucky man!

The Legend of Lylah Clare (1968)

I was reunited with Peter Finch and Bob Aldrich for this one, though it didn't work out as well as the others. Peter was playing a megalo-maniacal film director and Kim Novak was his protégée, a young starlet.

Kim had to wear a purple wig in the film, for reasons I don't re-member. Well, she hated it. She didn't like the cut, she didn't like the color. She didn't want to wear it. Now, I sort of understood where she was coming from. This woman's blond hair and her great beauty were her trademarks. She was feeling a little insecure, I think, at having them disguised. Also, there was some confusion in the film. Peter's character was supposed to be directing Kim in a film about his late wife, who was a big star in the thirties. There was some ambiguity about whether Kim was playing the actress or was a reincarnation of the ac-tress. I know it confused the hell out of me, but I was lucky. I did my scenes and skedaddled. I can only imagine what it did to poor Kim.

Finally, one day, she decided to take it out on the wig. She just wasn't going to wear it anymore.

Unfortunately, they'd shot a lot of scenes and those couldn't be redone. Besides, it was integral to the story. Aldrich had to bribe her. He painted her dressing room purple and got a purple rug leading into the set just so that she'd feel she wasn't freakish in that wig.

The picture was a stinker, one of the few Aldrich made, because no one ever did figure out what the hell the plot was about. Ultimately, though, great directors, like any artists, are remembered for their successes and not their failures. I'm happy to say Bob falls into that category.

Ice Station Zebra (1968)

This was the most expensive film I was in to date.

First of all, it was in Cinerama, the super-widescreen process that required super-large sets just to fill the screen. Second, a big chunk of it was set in the North Pole, where the heroes of the film were racing to recover a spy satellite before the Russians got it. That meant big sets that had to look like ice, which isn't something that they ordinarily have on a back lot. Third, there were a lot of expensive special effects in the film, which ranged from outer space to jet fighters racing through the skies to our submarine sliding below ice floes.

I played a real rat in the picture, a Russian spy. I did it with an accent, though I used a trick I'd learned from a language coach. I only accented every third word or so. Audiences would think the accent was continuous, but they'd be able to understand what I was saying a little clearer.

My costars were Rock Hudson, the great British star Patrick McGoohan—of *Secret Agent* TV fame—and Jim Brown. John Sturges was our director.

I know I've said that so-and-so was a wonderful guy, or this one was a real gentleman, but Rock was all that and more. Handsome, too, and a better actor than he was given credit for. He was never temperamental, rarely flubbed a line. His private life was not exactly a secret. There were rumors that he was being watched by the FBI during the late 1950s, when they were still looking for Communists and hoped to shake them out by blackmailing gay actors who showed up at Rock's house. I remember Burt Lancaster saying he'd gone to dinner there. Now, Burt wasn't gay, and when I asked if he was afraid what people would think, he just laughed.

"Ernie," he said, "I go to the opera too, but I don't sing."

It broke my heart when Rock got ill. Despite the way AIDS had ravaged his body—and his looks—he still went out to support his old friend Doris Day at the press conference launching her cable show, *Doris Day's Best Friends*.

Like *The Guns of Navarone* and *Where Eagles Dare*, *Ice Station Zebra* was based on a best-selling novel by Alistair MacLean. It wasn't as big a hit as those other movies (it's a little hard to follow the plot at times), but it made a pot of money and nabbed a couple of Oscar nominations. I made *Ice Station Zebra, The Legend of Lylah Clare,* and an unremarkable western called *Chuka* back-to-back after the cancellation of *McHale's Navy* in 1966.

I guess I was still employable.

 The Split (1968)

In 1968, I made one more film with Jim Brown. It was also my last film with him.

The Split was directed by Gordon Flemyng and the all-star cast included Diahann Carroll, Julie Harris, Gene Hackman, and Jack Klugman. It was based on a good Donald E. Westlake novel about a robbery during a big football game, after which the money goes missing. The thieves each think one of the others has the cash. Not a bad premise, right? Unfortunately, the characters are paper thin, scenes seem to be missing, and the movie is generally predictable.

I have two vivid memories of the movie. One is a scene where Jim Brown and I slugged it out. I actually got my head bashed in because he took things a little too seriously. Well, okay. Even Spence knocked out Clark Gable's teeth. The other memory is when I hurt my foot.

We were working on a ship down at the harbor in Los Angeles. I had complained about an electrical cable laying across the path where we had to run. I said if I tripped over this thing I was liable to get hurt. I did it a couple of times, running up a gangplank and hiding behind the deck house, and everything was fine—on my end, anyway. Jim was supposed to be coming after me.

The director kept calling "Cut."

I finally asked Mr. Flemyng, "What the hell is wrong?"

He said, in his very Scottish accent, "Well, Mr. Brown is trying to get his thing together."

I said, "Jesus, all he has to do is run after me!"

Well, Jim was famous for running when he played in the NFL.

Maybe he wanted to find a way of doing it differently, so people wouldn't think of him as Jim Brown the fullback. I don't know. All I know is that we did the scene again and again until finally I did step on this cable the wrong way and broke a bone in my left foot. I had to go to the hospital and Mr. Flemyng had to settle for a take that was already in the can. I had to do the rest of the picture in a cast, which the director artfully shot around so people wouldn't see it.

Echoing my own sentiments, Mr. Flemyng—who was a wonderful, decent, human being—went up to Jim on the last day of shooting.

"If you were the last actor on Earth," he said, "I would never work with you again."

Directors are people, too, you know.

Chapter 26

Back in the Saddle, Big-Time

Talk about a western!

The Wild Bunch, which I made in late 1968, ended up being one of the all-time greats, though it was not much fun to make. It was my first picture for director Sam Peckinpah. His vocabulary had increased beyond "okay," though there were times I wished it hadn't. Still, the results were worth it.

The story is simple: a bunch of bank robbers shoot up a town and are pursued to oblivion by the law. In Peckinpah's hands it became a masterpiece, an illustration of how the age of the gunfighter was giving way to civilization, and—of course—slow-motion bloodshed. And what a cast—William Holden, Robert Ryan, Ben Johnson, Warren Oates, Edmond O'Brien, Strother Martin, and L. Q. Jones.

At the age of fifty-one, I got to do more action scenes in this film than in any of my previous pictures.

At one point, after we had robbed this railroad office, we were supposed to make a dash for the horses under a rain of gunfire. My foot was still recovering from being busted in *The Split*, a fact that Sam had known for a while but only now addressed on the set.

"Shit," he said. "How the hell am I gonna get you through the field of fire to your horse?"

I said, "I can run a little bit."

He waved that idea away, but didn't have one to replace it.

I said, "What if I roll and shoot at the same time?"

Without another word, he went back to the camera, rolled, and said, "Action!"

I guess that meant "yes." So I threw myself to the ground and rolled across the street, *bam, bam.*

When I got onto the horse he said, "Okay, cut." Then he came over to me. "You son of a bitch," he said. "I should have thought of that."

As with many—actually, most—pictures, we never realized how great it would be while we were making it. I'll never forget the first time the picture was shown. It was in Jamaica at a big film festival that Warner Brothers threw. They flew in film critics from around the world to see five pictures. It was first class all the way, from fancy hotels to banquets.

One night they showed *The Wild Bunch.* The next morning they held a symposium where reporters could ask us questions. As we sat on this stage, the very first question out of the box was "Why was this picture ever made?"

We were astounded because we thought we'd done something pretty good.

Bill Holden asked, "What do you mean?"

The reporter said, "This is the blood-thirstiest film we've ever seen. It's terrible!"

We tried to explain that violence with a purpose is not gratuitous, it's art. We explained that Peckinpah was just portraying what really happens when people get shot. He was the first to do this, in fact. He was the first to show how people get shot from the front to the back, or the back to the front, and how the bullet comes out the other side in a spray of blood. *Pow!* It tore through you and you fell dead

(I don't dispute that *The Wild Bunch* was extremely violent—the climactic shootout took twelve days to film and more blank rounds were discharged than live rounds were fired during the Mexican Revolution of 1914. In total ninety thousand rounds were fired, all blanks. The onscreen body count is more than 150. *The Wild Bunch* was even bloodier than *Bonnie and Clyde,* which had been criticized harshly in 1967 for its violence.)

But it was no use. They'd already decided that the work and the people who made it were pretty much worthless.

We thought it better to just shut up and take our lumps. Well, the picture opened in the United States and I was astounded. Most of the critics—even some who had lambasted us—wrote, "This is one of the greatest westerns ever made."

Often, a viewer needs to let a picture sink in before making up his or her mind about it. That's one reason I've always been opposed to opening-night reviews of plays: sometimes a work of art needs to be digested before it is embraced or dismissed. It's not always like food, where you know right away that something is to your liking or not. Hell, how many years did it take for critics to decide that *Citizen Kane* is one of the greatest American films of all time? It didn't even win the Best Picture Oscar the year it was released.

William Holden, who did have a drinking problem, kept the boozing to a bare minimum, at least during the shoot. And he never came to the set inebriated. Part of that, he told me, was because he wanted to marry his girl, but she refused unless he gave up the bottle. He would stop for a while, but he couldn't control it. It was just too much for him, I guess. He died a dozen years later, falling and hitting his head during a bout with the bottle. What a useless, stupid way to go.

We had some great veteran actors on that film. Edmond O'Brien, who played crusty old Freddie Sykes, was half-blind at the time he made the film. He really had to work hard to hit his marks, but the old pro did it.

Like John Wayne, Ben Johnson was a real-life cowboy who'd

knocked around the industry since the 1940s. Also like Wayne, John Ford discovered him and had took him under his wing and put him in almost every movie he did. He could ride a horse. I mean, he could really ride a horse! He'd do anything the director asked and never complain no matter how long the hours were. A couple of years later, when he got his Academy Award for *The Last Picture Show*, he said, "You know something? I deserve this."

It brought down the house.

Warren Oates was someone Sam Peckinpah really liked, and he used him whenever he could. Like Lee Marvin, he was a former marine who was damn convincing in these all-man kind of roles. He was lean and wiry and very active, and I was stunned when we lost him to a heart attack at the age of fifty-three.

I'd worked with Robert Ryan before on *The Dirty Dozen* and in 1956 on *Bad Day at Black Rock*. Ryan was a stone-cold pro (and former marine). You'd never believe it looking at his weathered mug and six-foot-four frame that he'd once starred in *Antony and Cleopatra* with Kate Hepburn. You'd also never believe it, watching this two-fisted guy on screen, that he was a real pacifist at heart. He had guts: he stood up to McCarthy during the Red Scare, he marched for civil rights, and he was opposed to nuclear proliferation. It's usually the case, isn't it? The guys who have been to war understand why it's a last-resort kind of thing.

Jaime Sánchez was Angel, the youngest of the Wild Bunch. He was barely thirty at the time, and he was like a kid in a candy store. He just loved playing with his gun and he got to be a real fast draw. But it got to be irritating, having him constantly pull his six-shooter on us.

One day while we were waiting for Sam to call us, Holden stood up, took him by the neck, and said, "Put the goddamn thing in your holster and keep it there."

I backed him up, but poor Jaime had no idea where that was coming from. I think we were just privately pissed that he had more energy than the rest of us.

There's a scene near the end of the movie, right before the big shoot-out, where Bill Holden, Warren Oates, and Ben Johnson are enjoying one last fling in a whorehouse. I'm sitting outside, whittling a stick. I don't know how many people have asked me, "How come you weren't in the whorehouse, too?" I always respond, "How do you know I wasn't? Maybe I was finished."

It was a strange "bunch" of actors to be thrown together, but somehow our different methods and backgrounds all meshed on-screen. It's gratifying when that happens. It's even more gratifying when audiences respond.

Chapter 27

Things Go Downhill for a While

The Adventurers (1970)

It's not always fun and games. In fact, sometimes you think about giving it up and becoming a bricklayer.

The Adventurers was a big-screen soap opera directed by Lewis Gilbert, an Englishman, from the best-selling novel by Harold Robbins. Gilbert went on to do a bunch of James Bond films, and he had better luck with them.

The playboy son of an assassinated South American politician discovers that his father was a pretty rotten guy and decides to devote his life and fortune to saving his country. The key part was being played by a Yugoslavian actor named Bekim Fehmiu. I heard that he had been cast by the director's wife, who seemed to take a liking to him. He was pretty green, but he'd be getting strong support from people like Charles Aznavour, Alan Badel, Candice Bergen, Rossano Brazzi, Olivia de Havilland, Leigh Taylor-Young, John Ireland, and a bunch of others. We were loaded with talent. At least, where the cast was concerned.

To begin with, we were not exactly living like kings. We were shooting in Colombia, South America, and I had a little hut that was barely large enough for the four-poster bed. The bed's legs were stuck in cans filled with water so rats couldn't climb up.

Gilbert gave us a great pep talk when we started, saying, "Ladies and gentlemen, we're all in this together and we're going to get this picture done right."

Yeah, great. We were living like pigs while he was living in a fourteen-bedroom house with servants.

But that wasn't the worst of it. This was the first time I was ever thrown off a picture. I would occasionally make suggestions to this young man, Bekim, who didn't know his onions from anything. I was trying to be helpful but he just didn't understand the language and had apparently learned his lines phonetically. I mean, he obviously didn't understand when they asked him if he could drive, because he said, "Oh, yes." He took the car and wrecked it. And before you say, "Hey—didn't you do that with horseback riding?" there's a difference. I had a lot of help from the horse. This car couldn't drive itself.

I kept trying to work with him, but he was obviously getting frustrated. Finally, he went to the director and said that I was being difficult. The director said to me, "What have you done?"

I said, "What's the matter?"

"Bekim said you were giving him direction."

I said, "Are you nuts? I was trying to help him along in the scene!"

At which point—having gone from angry to livid because I'd called him "nuts"—the director said, "Get off my picture, get off my set!"

I walked off the set. I didn't want to go home because I'd never been fired from a movie. I went to my dressing room and stayed there.

Thank God for a very fine English actor by the name of Alan Badel, who went to Mr. Gilbert and cleared it up. I finished the film and was happy to get out of there. It was my worst experience in nearly twenty years of filmmaking.

The picture was shown for the very first time on the maiden flight of the first 747 that flew from New York to L.A.—and loaded with a bunch of newspaper columnists and an open bar.

Everybody got pissed to the ears. The next day the studio had to show the picture again because nobody remembered seeing it. I got some good notices, Bekim got fewer, and today the picture is kind of a camp classic.

I had the great good fortune of having Mr. Lewis Gilbert come up to me one time here in Hollywood and he said, "You know, Ernie. You made that picture. You were the best."

I said, "Thank you, Mr. Gilbert," and walked away.

Enough said.

Suppose They Gave a War and Nobody Came? (1970)

I'm not sure the movie really addressed the title question, though it did answer this one: *Suppose They Made a Movie and Nobody Came?*

This epic was a comedy about the conflict between an army base, run by Don Ameche, and a small Southern town, with me as the local sheriff. We had my buddy from *The Vikings*, Tony Curtis, along with Brian Keith, Suzanne Pleshette, Ivan Dixon, Tom Ewell, Bradford Dillman, and Arthur O'Connell, a fine cast.

I was glad to have it waiting for me when I got finished with *The Adventurers*. To tell you the truth, I'm not even sure I read the script before agreeing to do it.

My agent, said, "Here, you're going to make this picture."

I said, "Okay."

We had a lot of fun doing it and I got a paycheck, even though it turned out terrible. I also got to know dear, dear Suzanne Pleshette, another one we lost too soon. That's one thing about this business. You get to work closely with a lot of people. When you lose them, you really feel it. But you know—I feel privileged to have known most of these folks, so it's worth it in the end.

Bunny O'Hare (1971)

If you haven't figured it out by now, I loved and respected Bette Davis. It was quite a thrill to get together again for this picture in 1971. Honestly, we didn't know what the hell we were shooting, but had a wonderful time doing it.

Bette played a woman who had been thrown out of her home when the bank took it over. While she and the bankers were having a discussion in her house, I walked in and asked, "Where's the toilet?"

She said, "It's right around the corner." So I went around the corner and pretty soon I come out with the toilet on my shoulder.

She said "Where you going with my toilet?"

I said, "Mexico."

She said, "Mexico?"

I said, "What's the matter, you got something against Mexicans?"

You can see what kind of a picture this was. But Bette and I were game for "whacky."

My character took pity on this poor lady being thrown out of her home and let her sleep in the back of his truck, along with all the toilets I was taking to Mexico. Meanwhile, she finds out I was once a crook and convinces me to help her rob banks.

Sadly, the picture was not well edited and made no sense. Bette was so upset she wanted her name taken off it. I think she sued the producers. I told her, "Sue them for me, too."

Today, it has a cult following—something for which I'm grateful, even if I still don't understand it. But talk about a cult following . . .

Willard (1971)

In late 1970 I got a call from my agent, who said, "They want you for a picture named *Willard*."

I said, "What's it about?"

He said, "A young man who had a couple of hundred rats as pets."

I thought it was one of the nuttiest things I'd done. But it was a small hit and has a huge following all these years later. Bruce Davison starred as the title character, a nerd named Willard Stiles who has been forced out of his late father's company by my character. To make things worse, I keep him on the staff and humiliate him every chance I get. This was not *Ratatouille*, folks. At the end, Willard sends a horde of rat allies to kill those who have oppressed him—specifically me—before he's done in himself by the rats

You haven't lived until you've been covered with live rats. Even trained ones, like we used, are creepy as hell. Animal trainer Moe DiSesso had to smear me with peanut butter to get the rats to attack me. They aren't afraid of people and don't go running when you shoo them. I kept reminding myself that, unlike back in Queens, where we also had rats, at least now I was getting paid. If you've ever seen *Willard*, you'll note that the rats look like they were being tossed onto me, which is exactly how it was done. One of the rats got a little carried away and bit me. I had to get a tetanus shot. I think the rat got a shot, too.

For months after the filming, I had terrible nightmares about being attacked by rats. I actually woke up screaming more than once. Ah, the glamour of moviemaking.

We also had Elsa Lanchester in that one. She's probably best remembered as the Bride of Frankenstein in the 1935 film. She was a character, with a quick tongue and a bawdy sense of humor, but a really lovely lady. She was about seventy when she did the picture, and had more spunk than the rest of us combined.

Willard was a surprise smash hit when it was released in the summer of 1971, pulling in $6 million at the box office, a pretty nice piece of change at that time. I'd been offered a percentage of the profits, but once I read the script, I didn't think the movie would find much of an audience, so I opted for a higher salary instead. Live and learn.

The success of *Willard* inspired a sequel the following year. *Ben* was a flop, best remembered for the theme song sung by Michael Jackson!

Hannie Caulder (1972)

Hannie Caulder gave me a chance to work with one of the great western directors, Burt Kennedy, who had made hits like *The War Wagon* and *Support Your Local Sheriff*. This one starred Raquel Welch, Robert Culp, Jack Elam, Strother Martin, Christopher Lee, Diana Dors, and me. I'm the oldest of three brothers who come into a little town, mess up a robbery, and end up hiding at a little horse ranch where they discover Raquel Welch and her husband. We kill him, rape her, then get picked off one by one after a bounty hunter, played by Robert Culp, teaches her how to shoot.

Despite the rough subject matter, we all had fun on that picture. Raquel was—and still is—a breathtaking beauty, and she had great natural instincts. The actor who really shines, though, is Bob Culp. This guy is one of our great national treasures. Watch anything he ever does, whether it's *Bob & Carol & Ted & Alice* or *I Spy* on TV or a western like this. He's convincing in everything because, like Gary Cooper, he's one of the great listening actors of all time. I wish I had half of whatever he's got.

The picture didn't make much of a splash. It was an era of antiheroes, like we had in *The Wild Bunch*. Traditional westerns weren't the box-office successes that had once been.

I remember at one luncheon of the Hollywood Foreign Press Association, who should I be sitting across from but dear Raquel. I remember sitting there thinking, *Hey—I rolled her around in the hay, once.*

I hope nobody noticed me smiling.

🎬 *The Revengers* (1972)

This western was an attempt to return audiences to the dark territory of *The Wild Bunch* with a dash of *The Dirty Dozen*. We had Bill Holden again, and Daniel Mann—who'd directed *Willard*—tried real hard, but we didn't make it. The story was pretty straightforward. After his family is murdered by Indians, Bill's character, a rancher, goes to a prison camp and asks to borrow some of the prisoners to hunt them down. I was one of the volunteers. Woody Strode, a six-foot-four former athlete probably best remembered for his gladiator fight with Kirk Douglas in *Spartacus*, was another.

We made *The Revengers* in Parras, Mexico, the same place we made *The Wild Bunch*. It was pretty remote, and the people who lived in this little town did not know anything about anything. They were still playing westerns with Tom Mix and Buck Jones. That's how far behind they were. It broke my heart. At the time, the United States government was sending up these great big silver astronomical balloons from just across the border. The locals would see these huge silver things go by and run into their houses because they were frightened that it was the wrath of God.

I speak a little of the language, so I'd tell them *"No, es un globo grande"*—"It's a big balloon!" I explained it as best I could, told them about the stars and this and that. I tried to explain that even pictures came out of the sky, but they didn't understand. They didn't know what television was. All they knew was what they did for a living: they made overalls.

For a while, I had trouble with this picture. The first four days on location, I couldn't come up with a character. For one thing, I was worried about my marriage to my fourth wife, Donna. We didn't part under the most pleasant circumstances—in fact, the end of our marriage was pretty nasty. She took me for all I had, including the house. But her lawyer took her for a ride, too, and she ended up selling the house back to me, for $25,000, which was what she needed. When it comes to women, I guess I was too good to them, too honest. I found out a few times that you try your best, you try to do everything you possibly can for the woman you marry, and all they want is your money. Or they don't care about you, really—they just want to see what they can get out of you. I don't consider myself the most good-looking man in the world, but I always felt that my heart was on my sleeve, and maybe they took advantage of it. I was giving Donna $2,000 a month for the support of my two kids and one day I got a call saying the kids were starving and despite a court order my ex-wife was taking them out of the county.

Not long after the divorce, I went to pick up my kids, who were living with her. My little daughter said, "Daddy, we don't ever want to see you anymore!" I left the house and didn't see them for years. Donna had turned the children against me. My children and I have since reconciled, but it was a very painful time for me.

In *The Revengers*, we were trying to capture some of the glory we'd found in the Peckinpah film. But I wanted to make my work different some how.

After a couple of flat-footed scenes, the director, Daniel Mann looked at me and said, "What's the matter, Ernie?"

I said, "Gee, I'm sorry. I just can't seem to come up with something here."

He said, "That's all right, it'll work out."

That night at the hotel, I was just starting to call home and the telephone rang. It was my publicity man. He said, "Sit down, I've got some news for you."

I said, "What's the matter?"

He said, "Your wife just sued you for divorce."

I was hurt, I was shocked, but there was something else: I had my character. Then and there I decided to play my wife. You know, that wonderful person who turned around one day and told you what she really thought, that you were a dirty no-good this and that. That secret, what she was preparing behind my back, was the thing I couldn't put my finger on. I went back to the set the next day and it really came off.

Danny came over to me after a few takes and said, "My God, where'd you find him?"

I said, "A parting gift from my wife."

I really threw myself into the role after that. That's what you do, when the work is suddenly all you have. I think Bill Holden found my zeal a little intimidating, though. In one scene I took a flying header into a hole that I had dug to save myself from flying bullets. I had softened the landing by stacking a bunch of cartons in there—standard stuntman tactic. I really threw myself in there with great abandon. Bill followed me in.

When the dust settled, Bill lifted his head and said, "For Christ's sake, Borgnine, give us a break, will you?"

He didn't want to have to work so hard to keep me from showing him up. But it really was just a good-natured dig. He appreciated it when you forced him to pump up his own game.

 *Chapter 28*

Clowning Around

I was on the *Tonight Show* with Johnny Carson, promoting one of my films. For the record, there has never been a TV interviewer better than Johnny. He had no problem letting the guest have the spotlight, but if you got into trouble, couldn't think of anything to say, he was there with a question or quip to help you. Yet as outgoing as he was on camera, he was really quiet, even shy, backstage. I liked him an awful lot, though, and always enjoyed going on his show.

This night he said, "Ernie, you've done just about everything there is to do as an actor. What's left?"

After thinking a bit, I said, "Well, let's see. I've never been a clown."

He said, "Boy, you're going to get letters."

Sure enough, the very next day a fellow by the name of Ben Barkin called me from Milwaukee and said, "You want to be a clown? We'll make you the head clown in our circus parade. It's going to be the greatest circus parade in the world. We go on July the 14th."

Well, how do you say no to something like that?

I flew to Milwaukee. Ben Barkin brought in a clown from Ringling Brothers. He put makeup on me, just enough to show that I was a clown, yet left enough of Ernie showing so that people would still know I was the guy from *McHale's Navy*.

Ben had some vintage circus wagons brought in on a big train through Chicago. It was quite an event. They set up the whole circus spectacle and all those beautiful wagons were on display. On Sunday, when we put on the parade, it was just the most colorful, epic, exciting thing you could imagine. There was just one problem: crowd-wise, it was pretty much of a bust. I don't think we had more than 15,000 people on the streets. We'd see one person and wave like crazy.

I'd say from the side of my mouth, "Oh boy, there's a fan."

But Ben was undeterred. He said, "We're going to do better next year," and he did. I appeared in the parade from 1972 until 2002. That last year I did it, we had over 2 million people watching along the route. And it got me thinking. I think it would be great if politicians put on a clown outfit every now and then and really got to know the people. You would be surprised what you can see in people's eyes when you're a clown. They look upon you as a person who is bringing a little joy into their lives. That's what I felt, and I treasured it. I remembered it every time I made a film. If a president or senator or governor could remember that look, that sense of responsibility, whenever they made a decision, the world would be a better place. In fact, if politicians wore clown makeup on the job, maybe they'd fight a little less among themselves.

Just a thought, humbly submitted for your consideration.

Chapter 29

The Poseidon Adventure (1972)

Marty was my Oscar winner. *The Wild Bunch* was my classic. But *The Poseidon Adventure* was a box-office colossus and the one everybody seems to remember and asks about. I have to say, it's one of the most personally satisfying films I've made.

The script was based on a novel by Paul Gallico—who while onboard ship to England wrote the book in two days. It caught the eye of Irwin Allen. As most of you know, it's about ten passengers who struggle to survive after their ocean liner is capsized by a big wave.

Until he made this film, Irwin was best known for his science fiction TV series *Voyage to the Bottom of the Sea* and *Lost in Space*. He'd made a couple of features, but nothing the size and scope of this one.

I've known a lot of filmmakers in my day, but none of them was a master showman like Irwin. He was an intense, active man with wiry hair and absolutely no pretension. He was the most unmogul-mogul you could imagine. He was like Cecil B. DeMille in the sense that he knew what audiences wanted to see, he served it up big, and he knew how to sell it. His next film, *The Towering Inferno*, was an even bigger hit.

The man was amazing. He was also very, very considerate of his actors. I know that some of my costars complained that this was a tough shoot, but they knew the story when they came aboard. For me, compared to *The Adventurers*, this was fun! Irwin always made sure the water was not too cold, and had bunches of towels and blankets waiting for us if we had a scene in the water. When there were mechanical effects—floors tilting, pianos falling, things exploding—he put safety above everything else. The main ballroom set was built on these big hydraulic lifts that tilted it as far as forty-five degrees or so.

If there were stunt people in the scene—and sometimes there were more than a hundred of them—Irwin and his team made sure every prop was rigged with wires so they'd fall where he wanted them to go. If the stunt people had to take a tumble, he personally watched to make sure they knew what was going to happen and how they were going to handle it.

Some people I've worked with, like Peckinpah, pretty much had you go in and take your chances. He made you feel less manly for taking precautions, like putting something soft under the dirt if you had to fall off a horse. Not Irwin or the English gentleman who was directing our film, Ronald Neame. However, I can't say that everything worked perfectly. One day when the set was supposed to tilt a little, then stop, it didn't stop. The camera crew were thrown in the water and Irwin shouted, "Save the film!"

He was only half-joking. Some crew members pulled the camera operators out while others saved the film magazine. Irwin had it developed ASAP, to make sure they wouldn't have to shoot the expensive scene again.

Irwin was particularly generous to me. Remember, Irwin had never made a really big picture before. Movies like *The Lost World* and *Five Weeks in a Balloon* did a lot of their business back then in what were called the "kiddie matinees." At night, theaters often showed something else. Irwin had no track record making big budget movies.

The Poseidon Adventure was a story he fell in love with, though, and he knew it was his ticket to the major leagues. He bought the rights to the novel with his own money and started casting it before he had a start date firmly in place. He knew who he wanted and he didn't want to lose them; at least one actor, Gene Wilder, had already turned him down because of a scheduling conflict. Irwin later brought in Red Buttons for the role, and he was terrific.

Irwin wasn't worried. He'd been making movies and TV shows for 20th Century-Fox for ten years. He was sure they'd back him.

I went to meet him in his office at Twentieth Century-Fox. He said, "Listen. I'm going to put you under contract until we make this film. I'm not sure when the cameras are going to roll, but I don't want you in Timbuktu when they do. It shouldn't be more than a couple of weeks."

So he paid me a generous salary while I sat at home on my keister. He did the same with Red Buttons. Unfortunately, Irwin's generosity almost got him in big trouble. During that time, the studio was in the midst of a takeover crisis. They'd lost a fortune years before on *Cleopatra,* and had to pay off that debt by selling a big chunk of the back lot to real estate developers. They'd lost another bundle more recently on the war film *Tora! Tora! Tora!* For Twentieth Century-Fox, the era of big-budget films was over. When Irwin went over to pay his respects to the new chief, he was told, "Stick to TV. We're not going to do your picture."

Irwin went back to his office in shock. Ronnie Neame happened to be there.

Ronnie said, "What's wrong?"

Irwin told him.

Ronnie said, "Do you have a bottle of whiskey here?"

Irwin said, "Yes."

Ronnie said, "Well, let's have a couple of shots and we'll go over and talk to him."

So they had their shots and went over to talk to the new studio head.

This guy was no idiot. He liked the idea, just not the budget, which was in the neighborhood of $10 million. Finally, he looked over and he said, "I'll tell you what. You put up half the money and we'll make the picture."

Unfazed, Irwin left the Fox offices and merely walked across the street to a country club where a couple of his friends were playing golf. One of them was Steve Broidy, who had an outfit called Allied Artists for years. Allied Artists specialized in low-budget bread-and-butter pictures like westerns and horror movies and the very successful Bowery Boys series. Irwin had made *The Big Circus* with Victor Mature and Rhonda Fleming for Allied in 1959 and the picture made a fortune.

Broidy guaranteed Irwin the $5 million right on the spot, between the nineth and tenth holes, and *The Poseidon Adventure* was back on track.

Irwin was clever about cutting corners to bring the picture in on budget. Unless you know, you can't see where corners were cut. He still spent everything he wanted on the big scenes, like the banquet hall (where Carol Lynley lip-synched the huge Oscar-winning hit song "The Morning After," which made more, I'm sure, than the entire budget of our film). But other shots were the kind of sleights of hand Irwin had learned working on low-budget TV fare. For instance, in the last shot, where you were supposed to see the overturned ship surrounded by rescue vessels, all you see is a piece of the hull with a helicopter in the distance. That was shot right on the studio lot, with the camera angled so you couldn't see the soundstages.

The Poseidon Adventure was fourteen weeks of backbreaking work, but we had our fun, too. I remember watching Shelley Winters and Jack Albertson playing cards. She lost about $130,000 to Jack, and then refused to pay him. That was her only loss, by the way: she had to gain about thirty pounds to play the part of Jack's wife Belle. She wasn't happy about either of those things, but she was game about doing as many of her own underwater stunts as Ronnie would allow.

Gene Hackman, who starred as the priest who leads us to safety, was a bit of a surprise. The very first morning, we were doing a scene on the *Queen Mary*—which was doubling for our ship, another of Irwin's cost-saving moves—and Gene had a few lines. He and I rehearsed a little before the cameras rolled. He stumbled a little and I asked him if everything was okay. He looked over at me and said, "Are we supposed to know this stuff?"

I said, "Well, yeah. That's the general idea."

He looked at me rather oddly. "Really," he said as if that were a divine revelation. He had just made that wonderful picture, *The French Connection*, that had won him the Academy Award. He told me they kind of made up that picture as they went along, He thought the same thing was going to happen in *The Poseidon Adventure.*

"No," I said. "Irwin really likes the script as it's written."

I didn't mean it to be offensive or anything, but he never spoke to me again except in the business of making the picture. He was excellent in the part and was a great guy to work with. But he didn't say too much to anybody.

After the picture was finished on-time and on-budget, a very grateful Irwin Allen threw a party along with the president of Twentieth Century-Fox (the same executive who'd tried to cancel it). My wife, Tova, whom I'd married in early 1973 (more about that later) loudly predicted that the film would make at least $200 million worldwide. The studio brass smiled indulgently, but she was right.

To top it off, the studio sent the cast on a promotional trip, shuttling us from Norway to France to Spain to Germany and to Italy. Everywhere we went the picture was huge, the biggest phenomenon Twentieth Century-Fox had ever seen. And its popularity continues to this day. Recently, I've been giving lectures about the movie business on cruise ships, where they always show *The Poseidon Adventure.*

It always shakes everybody up because, thanks to Irwin, it looks like the real McCoy.

Funny thing. The picture was remade a few years back for darn near what our picture earned, and with state-of-the-art special effects. Guess which version audiences like better? (You bet I'm proud of that one!)

I admit that I haven't seen the remake. I heard it was pretty good, at least from the technical and special effects end. However, I think today's filmmakers could have learned a thing or two from Irwin Allen. Irwin believed in loading his movies with the big stars of the day and casting familiar faces in smaller roles. *The Poseidon* remake had some great actors—my pal Kurt Russell and Richard Dreyfuss—but it didn't, from what I heard, take much time to develop any of the characters. So when they start dying off, the audience doesn't really care. State-of-the-art special effects are great, but the audience has to have an emotional investment in the people onscreen. Who didn't cry when Shelley Winters dies after rescuing Gene Hackman or when Stella Stevens falls into the pit of fire?

That's my two cents.

Chapter 30

Havin' More Fun

 Emperor of the North (1973)

Before I talk about the movie, there's a story I have to tell about Sam Peckinpah. I had agreed to do *Emperor of the North* while I was still shooting *The Poseidon Adventure*.

Sam was supposed to direct *Emperor of the North* and was really keen to do it, but he lost his option to Bob Aldrich. Even though Sam had made a bunch of hit films since *The Wild Bunch*—including *Straw Dogs* and *The Getaway*—he couldn't make *Emperor* for as little as the studio wanted to spend. Well, by now you know what the situation was with Fox and money. He couldn't get them to budge.

One day, I stopped by Sam's office on the Fox lot.

I said, "Sam, how are you?"

Sam mumbled something. He was obviously thinking about something else.

I said, "Quick question. Can you give me any pointers about this *Emperor of the North*? Any ideas on how I should play the part?"

He said, "Get the hell out of here."

Evidently, Sam was a little teed off about his losing the picture. I understood why he was upset and his attitude didn't bother me. I was used to it. But it underscored a big difference between him and me. People often want things that somebody takes away from them or that just don't happen for some reason. My attitude has always been that there are other opportunities around the corner and that holding a grudge or being bitter is counterproductive. Even with directors I've disliked or former wives who gave me a pain—I never sat around thinking, *I'm gonna get you* or *Jeez, I want to see them fall on their ass.* I believe that you get back from life what you put out, so I always try to show respect and compassion.

I finished *The Poseidon Adventure* on a Friday night, spent Saturday at home packing, and left on Sunday to go to Portland, Oregon, to make *Emperor of the North* with Aldrich and, once again, my pal Lee Marvin. We also had Keith Carradine and some of the finest veteran character actors in the business—Simon Oakland, Charlie Tyner, and Elisha Cook, Jr., whom you may remember as Sydney Greenstreet's evil henchman in *The Maltese Falcon.*

Based on a short story by Jack London, "Emperor of the North Pole" is the title given to the head hobo of any group who rides the rails. The studio was afraid no one would know what the heck that meant, so it was shortened to *Emperor of the North,* as if that makes any more sense. You know, sometimes studios sell audiences short. If you give people a title they don't quite get, it doesn't mean they'll walk away. They may just be interested enough to find out what it's all about!

I played a railroad conductor named Shack, the most evil, sadistic scoundrel who ever existed. Nobody rode my train without a ticket, and nobody had tickets because this was a freight train. And I didn't want any hobos on my train—it's a point of honor for my character. No one even attempts to go on my train—except Lee, who let it be known that he is going to try.

He throws me off my own train at the end.

When I arrived on the set on Monday morning, Bob Aldrich was standing in front of the train. This was a real train, of course, not a set. He asked me, "Ernie, have you ever worked on a train before?"

I said, "No."

He said, "Well, there's the engine."

"Yes."

"And that's the caboose."

"Yes."

"You will be working all of it, from the engine to the caboose. You've been working on this train for thirty years, so you better familiarize yourself with it."

I said, "Yes."

He said, "Okay, go get dressed." As I started off he gave me just about the only direction he would provide. "Oh, and remember," he said, "don't look down when you run on top of the train."

"Running on top?" I asked. Usually, those kinds of shots are done with special effects or stuntmen. Not this time.

He said, "Running on top, from the engine to the caboose, while it's moving."

I said, "Yes, sir."

That sounded a little dangerous, so I developed a character based on the actor Jack Elam, who I'd worked with on *Vera Cruz* and *Hannie Caulder*. Jack was walleyed. Imitating him, I tried to keep one eye looking straight ahead and the other eye down on the ground. I worked on muscle control in my trailer. I found out, though, that being on top of a moving train wasn't the only problem. It was only going twenty-five to thirty-five miles an hour, which wasn't so bad, but it rattled like an old bag of bones. All the nails would come loose on top and I was afraid I'd trip and impale myself. My footing wasn't so great to begin with, since they gave the characters leather shoes to run around outside with. That is not the kind of gripping surface you want on a moving train! To be on the safe side, before each shot, I actually went along with a hammer and whacked in the loose nails.

My character had a piece of lead about a foot long attached to a clothesline. Standing on top of the train, I'd play it out so that it would hit the tracks and ties and bounce underneath the train to dislodge any hoboes who were riding the rods underneath the cars. One time I was letting it out while the camera car was following on the road along-side. Suddenly, I looked up and saw that the camera car had stopped. I leaned over to see what was up. That clothesline had caught in the wheel, and the train was still moving. I let go just as it pulled me down, right over the side. I caught the last rung of a ladder that was there and hung on for dear life until the train came to a stop. I was shak-ing, I have to admit. I remember thinking that they couldn't pay me enough to do real stunt work for a living!

I should probably mention that those folks who risk life and limb are pretty well paid. There was one stuntman doubling for Gary Cooper and Burt Lancaster on *Vera Cruz*. He had to do this jump over a chasm. It was about a thousand feet down and he jumped the horse twice, once dressed as Coop, once as Burt. He got $1,000 every time he did it. He earned every nickel.

I didn't get any extra hazard pay for *Emperor of the North*. Frankly, I wouldn't have taken ten times my salary to do that kind of stuff.

The picture only did okay business at the box office. I don't think the public knew quite what to make of it. Still, it remains one of my favorites to make and one of my favorites to watch.

The Neptune Factor (1973)

When a studio has a hit, somebody else inevitably tries to make the same picture again, on the cheap and in a hurry. Hollywood moguls always hope that lightning will strike twice. It rarely does, but they keep trying.

With *The Poseidon Adventure* lining 'em up at the box office, a bunch of investors put together one about a submarine that has to res-cue workers trapped in an undersea lab following an earthquake. Hey, I'm not being critical here. Producers are in business to make money, and not everything has to come from the heart or be a work of art. Me? As long as I'm having fun, that's enough.

I was having breakfast on Sunset Boulevard one morning when in came producer Sandy Howard, a friend of mine. He was about half-drunk. He said, "Damn it, I've got a picture shooting and you'd be perfect in it."

I said, "Then how come I'm not in it?"

He said, "You are now. But first I got to find a goddamn director."

Seems they were having problems with whoever had been engaged and had to replace him. A lot of submarine footage had been shot up in Canada—where it was cheaper to build sets and hire crews; it still is, in fact. Unfortunately, the lighting was unrealistic and the special effects showing the ocean outside the portholes of the lab were terrible. That would explain Sandy's half-drunkenness.

I said, "You want a real good director? I got one for you. His name is Dan Petrie."

Dan had directed me on TV years before and I thought highly of him. He was a good director, very encouraging.

Sandy said, "Daniel Petrie, okay. I'll find him."

Sure enough, he found him and we went ahead and made the picture with Ben Gazzara, Yvette Mimieux, and the great Walter Pidgeon playing one of the old scientists. We went back to Canada, where we had the same problems as they did on the first shoot.

I swear, we ended up making that picture three times before they got it right!

It's not bad, though I doubt it's on anyone top ten favorite movie list. I'm glad I got to work with Mr. Pidgeon, who died shortly after we finished. We exchanged stories about Irwin Allen, Mr. Pidgeon having played the lead in the film version of *Voyage to the Bottom of the Sea*. And Yvette—what a doll. I swear, I've spent more time with beautiful women than a guy with a kisser like mine has any right to. And I get paid for it.

Legend in Granite (1973)

In 1973, Universal producer Jon Epstein asked me to play the part of Coach Vince Lombardi, legendary coach of the Green Bay Packers, in a television movie.

He said, "Are you interested?"

I said, "Sure, I'll take a crack at it."

I felt cautious because I'd be playing someone who was not only known to so many people but also beloved by the people of Green Bay. I really had to get it right, or I'd take a lot of flak.

They fitted me out with a pair of glasses and a kind of widow's peak and the resemblance was pretty astonishing. I didn't know what the fans would say, but when I walked on the set I felt like the coach. Fortunately, my faith was not misplaced. On the first day of shooting we were on the field setting up. Paul Hornung, the Packers' star player, was an adviser on the picture. I walked up behind him and the director said to Hornung, "Oh, and you know the coach."

When he turned around and stared me in the face, he nearly fell down.

He said, "Jesus Christ, I buried him six months ago."

For me, the role turned out to be one of the easiest things I'd ever done. I had studied the newsreel footage, so I knew how he behaved on the field. I just carried that personality with me and did the rest the way I thought Lombardi would be.

For a couple of years after it was made, *Legend in Granite* was broadcast whenever Green Bay was going to play some other big team, or when they were up for another title. Since then, though, I've tried to get a copy, but it's locked away in a vault somewhere for reasons no one seems to recall. I'm guessing there are rights issues, but I sure wish it was available again.

Chapter 31

Tova

I was in the midst of getting a divorce in 1972 when my good friend, comedian Marty Allen, and his wife, Frenchy, invited me to his birthday party.

They said, "You've got to bring a girl."

I said, "Are you kidding? I'm through with women. As a matter of fact, I'm thinking of taking up with men."

They laughed and said, "We've got a wonderful girl for you. We're going to set you up on a blind date."

I said, "Do you have to?"

They told me, "Yes." They said I had to go pick up this lady who was in from Las Vegas and staying at one of the Beverly Hills hotels. I went over and evidently she was zigging while I was zagging, because we missed each other. I went back to Chasen's, where they were having the party,

I said to Marty, "You see? As far as women are concerned I'm a dead man. I can't even find my blind date."

Marty said, "She's coming by taxi. Everything will be fine."

So I was sitting there with all the rest, enjoying the party, when in came this great-looking redhead. I remember thinking, *Why can't my date look like her?*

Of course, it was her. We were introduced. Her name was Tova.

We found ourselves talking, she and I. We just kept talking and ignored everyone else at the party. It was like we'd known each other all our lives.

Finally, the party was over and I took her to her hotel and said good night. As I said good night I started to walk away and I said, "Oh, by the way . . ."

By that time she was already in the elevator. She stepped on the elevator operator's toes and said, "Don't you dare close that door yet."

I said, "By the way . . . what?'"

She said, "You forgot to ask me out again."

I laughed: "Jimmy Durante is having his fiftieth anniversary party over in Las Vegas and seeing as how you're from Las Vegas, would you mind if I called on you?"

She said, "That would be wonderful."

Later on, she admitted that she went back to her room and let out a whoop. She said she knew she had me hooked like a fish—and, I told her, I didn't mind at all being caught.

I went to Las Vegas and I picked her up at her home. I met her stepdad and her mother, one of the greatest gals in the world. Her name was Aase. After I got to know her better, I called her pain in the Aase and she just adored it.

Tova and I went out that evening and we had a wonderful time. One thing led to another and, damn, the first thing you know we were going steady. The second thing you know I proposed marriage. That did it.

Here we are, thirty-five years later, and we're still in love with each other. Oh, we've had our ups and downs, believe me, but she's a patient lady and she knows how much I love her. It's a mutual feeling of understanding and companionship. She's also a real go-getter, having turned her ideas about skin care into a thriving business.

Tova's son, David Johnson, has become a wonderful friend. I think of him as a son, as if he was my own. He's a computer genius and a talented musician. He's a wonderful guy.

Thanks, hon. Thanks for all of it!

Chapter 32

This 'n' That

 Twice in a Lifetime

Television had changed in the five-plus years since we'd stopped doing *McHale's Navy*. TV movies like *Legend in Granite* were quality productions and made the studios money through repeat viewings and being sold overseas for theatrical release. And, of course, TV series were making an absolute fortune in syndication—sold to local stations for rerun after their network runs had ended.

Newly married to my dear Tova, I was eager to stay home for a while. Over the years, every producer in town seemed determined to come up with a seagoing idea for me, something to rival the popularity of *McHale's Navy*. One of these actually got made, but was never picked up for a series. It was called *Twice in a Lifetime*, and had me as a tugboat skipper with Della Reese as my partner. We also had Arte Johnson of *Rowan & Martin's Laugh-In* fame, Slim Pickens, and what I thought was a really great script. Seemed like a natural, but it didn't sell to the front office. To this day, I don't know why.

 *Law and Disorder* (1974)

Sounds like that hit series that's on the air now, doesn't it?

It wasn't. This was one of those movies that came and went.

In late 1974 I went to New York City to make *Law and Disorder*, with Carroll O'Connor, who was as hot as a pistol from playing Archie Bunker on the groundbreaking sitcom *All in the Family*. Carroll played a cabbie and I was his best friend, who owned a beauty salon. We lived in a rough area of New York where the crime was out of control, so we formed an auxiliary police force. Not a bad premise, and not a bad movie. Sometimes, though, things just don't click.

My most vivid recollection of this one was our director, Ivan Passer, having a terrible time trying to keep everything together. Shooting on location can be a bear, and this was an important film for Carroll, who was trying to make it back to the big screen after his success on television. Most people don't remember that he had been in movies like *Lonely Are the Brave* and *Cleopatra* before settling in that easy chair as Archie Bunker. Carroll was a little anxious, and a little controlling as a result. Whenever anything went wrong, Ivan would come to me and say, "What should I do, Ernest?"

I always tried to smooth things out by staying cool

I remember one day he came to me, really upset. "Ernest," he said, "you know how this scene calls for just you and Carroll?"

I said, "Yes, that's right."

He said, "Well, Carroll wants his son and his wife in the scene, and they don't belong."

I said, "Well, couldn't they make a pass in the background?"

Ivan said, "No, no, he wants them to have lines."

His reason might have been more than just trying to get them exposure. When you talk on camera, you make more money.

Well, what do you do? Carroll and I talked and we ran the scene— once with and once without his family. He then saw the difficulty of giving them dialogue. He agreed that his wife and son couldn't be worked in.

I don't know where Ivan used them, but if you look really close you'll see Carroll's wife and son in there someplace.

Other than that, my most vivid recollection of this film was bloody knees. There was one scene where I was supposed to jump on the bed with actress Anita Dangler, who played my wife. Doing take after take with bare knees rubbed them raw and the next morning it was all I could do to wear pants. It was worth it, though—the scene played beautifully.

Yeah, I know. Poor me, having to jump into bed over and over with a beautiful lady!

 ## Little House on the Prairie (1974)

In 1974 I was approached by Michael Landon's casting director, Susan Sukman McCray, to do an episode of *Little House on the Prairie*. I read the script and said, "This is too sappy." Shows you what I know! I didn't want to do it at first, but they talked me into it. I'm glad they did, because it was one of the greatest experiences in my life. It was nice being back on the Universal back lot—boy, it had grown since the days of *McHale's Navy*, and the tour was now organized with military precision and was real big business! After being over at Fox, which had shrunk, this was a real shocker. Plus, I loved working with Mike Landon, who was one of the nicest and most generous men I've met in this business. What a loss when he died so young.

The episode was entitled "Old Man of the Mountain." On the show, Michael's daughter, played by Melissa Gilbert, had run away. She made her way to a mountain and met up with a mountain man— who was me. Her family was going crazy because they didn't know where she went and Michael started following a stream to see if he could find her. In the meantime, I taught her how to take care of a wounded dove and how to make a little cross and all kinds of stuff to survive in the wilderness.

The cross accidentally—or maybe on purpose—fell into the water and went down the river. Sure enough, Michael saw it and followed the stream and found his daughter. As he looked around, she said, "Dad, the man who helped me was here." But no one was there.

Who could it have been?

The Devil's Rain (1975)

What I was saying before about the Hollywood attitude of if-it-works-do-it-again certainly applies here.

The Exorcist was one of the biggest box-office smashes of all time and with its success came a lot of imitations. *The Devil's Rain* was one of them. Not that it was a cheap rip-off like some of the others. It had solid production values and a decent script. Producer Sandy Howard, for whom I did *The Neptune Factor*, assembled an amazing cast: William Shatner, Ida Lupino, Tom Skerritt, Eddie Albert, Keenan Wynn, and an unknown Italian kid from New Jersey making his film debut, John Travolta, who played my son.

The story started three centuries ago, when my character, Jonathan Corbis, led a coven of witches. Ancestors of the Preston family had betrayed Corbis and his Satanists by concealing their sacred book. For hundreds of years, the Prestons have been able to keep the book, without which Corbis is unable to deliver the souls to Satan. The title refers to the inundation which the witches use to melt people. In the end, it causes me to go the way of the Wicked Witch of the West.

The thing I remember the most is putting on the devil makeup for the climactic scenes. It took about four-and-a-half hours to make me up. A little Mexican boy in the film took a liking to me. He thought I was the greatest, like his favorite uncle or something. I told him the first day that we were going to put on this makeup and I couldn't be distracted, so I said, "Now you come back in about four hours, okay?"

So he came back and I turned around. You know, in my own head I'm still Ernie Borgnine. Well, he looked at me, let out one scream, and went running. And he never came back to see me.

I'll never forget that makeup, because I didn't have a lot of mobility. While it was on, I could only fork in a little rice and peas and beans, stuff like that, for lunch. Even so, food would drop into one of the nooks and crevices without my knowing it. So I'd be shooting a scene and doing dialogue and there would be a rice grain or two that would come flying out.

Bill Shatner was a hoot. He has a kind of florid style, as do I, and he's just so entertaining to watch on the set and on the screen. At the time, he was trying to slip out from under the shadow of the character he played on *Star Trek*, Captain Kirk, and not having a lot of success. The show was a huge hit in syndication and that was how he was known. Guys like him and Adam West, who was *Batman*, became icons who were hired *because* they reminded audiences of beloved characters and personalities.

John Travolta had a relatively small part, but he had star quality. Six-foot-two with boyish good looks and a great smile, he was pretty shy, but that's okay—a lot of actors are. But when the camera was on, he just lit up. I'm so glad for his success, and I appreciate the fact that unlike some stars who make it big, he doesn't go around bad-mouthing the kind of odd movies they often make when they're starting out (like me as a Chinese man). He's a class act all around.

Shoot (1976)

We went up to Canada to make this film about a National Guard group who go hunting together and have a beer fest. While they're out there, they encounter another band of hunters. One thing leads to another and the groups end up at war.

It was a mess from the word go. The picture was never shown in this country. According to the producer, the National Rifle Association paid the distributor not to release it. Who knows? Not me. I was just a hired gun, so to speak.

Cliff Robertson was my costar, and we had fun talking about his passion, which was flying. Cliff was another guy who started out in TV and made it big and we bonded over that. We had something else in common: he'd won the Best Actor Oscar in 1968 for *Charly*, and it hadn't done him a lot of good, either. Here we were, in the boonies, making this silly thing. But I'm not complaining. We cashed the checks and did our best. Cliff's still at it, too; he played Uncle Ben in the Spider-Man movie. I like Cliff.

I'll never forget one of the funny things that happened.

Some manufacturer had come out with a series of stones that had sayings on them. You were supposed to carry them around or put them in your pocket and remind yourself how lucky you were, or not to miss an opportunity, or some such.

I happened to be walking to the set one day out in the wilderness and I saw this perfectly round stone. I picked it up and decided to introduce it as my personal advisor, Harry.

They looked at it and then at me like I flipped. But pretty soon, everyone was coming over and asking Harry for advice on how to play this scene or that, or where to invest their money. And they'd listen and pretend he was answering.

I was carrying Harry in my pocket in a scene where we were supposed to investigate a shed of some kind. But we were afraid there was a minefield, so we had to trip the explosives.

The director was trying to figure out the perfect thing to use, and I said, "I've got it! Harry."

He said, "Who's Harry?"

I said, "Him"—and pulled out the stone.

In the picture you will actually see the stone being thrown, which is Harry. Goofy? Hell, yeah. Goofy is what movies are sometimes all about!

Chapter 33

Back in the Sandals Again

 Jesus of Nazareth (1977)

I went back to the distant past for my next project. Not in a toga, but as a Roman centurion in Franco Zeffirelli's 1977 epic *Jesus of Nazareth*. Franco is the man who gave us the classic *Romeo and Juliet*, among other great films.

This was my first TV miniseries. It was shot in Tunisia and we had an amazing cast. Robert Powell was Jesus, and we also had Tony Quinn, Anne Bancroft, Laurence Olivier, Claudia Cardinale, James Mason, James Earl Jones, and Christopher Plummer—in other words, "the works"! It turned out to be one of the best pictures of its kind. It was pious without being like a Sunday school class, and powerful without being over-the-top-bloody, if you catch my meaning.

Franco was a terrific director. He didn't do much direction. He just made a little adjustment here or there, mostly toning things down. He trusted his actors. He also loved Tova's soap. My wife had started a cosmetics line that was heavily advertised on TV and turned into a real industry. Franco liked the soap because where we were shooting the water was so hard that you couldn't get up lather. Tova's soap would foam up in the hardest water you could imagine.

Working in a foreign location with actors who often have thick accents is a chore. Local regulations require that local actors have to be used for smaller roles, but their English usually isn't up to snuff and they have to be dubbed later on. For that reason, to save money, producers don't bother recording sound on locations. They just have us come in and dub it later. Because there's no recording, the sets tend to be very noisy with people yelling and construction workers hammering and trucks coming and going. It is incredibly difficult to concentrate.

One thing that stands out vividly on this shoot were all the animals we had, and all the animal smells. It was pretty awful. I know the beasts gave Franco a hard time, all the donkeys, giraffes, elephants, and things you wouldn't believe. It seemed like every time you turned around, one animal wanted to attack another. (The well-endowed donkeys were ready to go at it with the giraffes.) Franco was yelling in Italian *"Vada, eliminili!"*—"Take them away!" and he would push them. No wonder he needed soap at the end of the day!

My first scene in this picture was when I, a great Roman warrior, went to ask Jesus to cure one of my servants, who was dying. As I started to beg, an extra ran up and said, "You should see your man, he's well, he's alive, he's happy." I looked back at this man, with his piercing blue eyes, and for a moment I was literally transported. For that second, he was Jesus Christ. It passed quickly, but it was one of the most surreal experiences I've had on a shoot. Not *the* most incredible, however. That was still to come.

I had a scene where I was looking up at Jesus after he'd been nailed to the cross. My preparation for this was pretty soul-searching. My feeling as the centurion was, "I've been in the army for a long time, but I don't like what I see. This man actually saved my servant, and now look what they're doing to him. I'm going to get out of the army."

The shot required the cameras to be looking down on me. Jesus was not in the frame. But it was important and Franco wanted me to get it right. So he said, "I'm not going to put the actor up on the cross."

I said, "No, just put a dot up there. I'll be able to work from that, Don't worry about it." I didn't want Powell to have to go up there.

So they put a mark where I was supposed to look and they had a camera right alongside it. They had another camera over on the other side, another camera behind me, looking down on me, and a fourth one behind the cross. Some directors like to have a lot of choices when they get in the editing room. It's better to have too much footage than not enough.

When everything was set, I said to Franco, "Would somebody please read what Jesus said on the cross: 'Forgive them for they know not what they do.'"

Franco said, "I will say it."

So we started. I was looking up at this dot on the cross as Franco said the words and, so help me, I actually saw the face of the Lord. A moment later his face dropped down over his shoulder and he was dead.

Tears as big as teacups came from my eyes, I swear to God. I started bawling like a baby. I just stood there with the tears coming down. Finally I heard "Cut."

I came back to reality, to the realization that we were actually making a picture.

Franco said, "Ernesto?"

I choked out, "Yes."

He said, "That was wonderful. Now, Ernesto, do you think you can do it one more time with less tears?"

I wanted to kill him. He had something real on film, and now he wanted me to fake it. Well, he was the director. In the finished film viewers see pieces from both takes. Though they almost didn't see any of them.

General Motors was sponsoring the show for Easter and when they saw the picture, they didn't want to show me crying. I don't know why. Maybe they thought it was a knock at the military, having a soldier cry. Or maybe they thought it was a little too reverent. I don't know. But the Vatican came back and said, "If you don't have the part in, we won't sanction the picture."

It stayed in the film.

 ## *The Greatest* (1977)

I got to play another real-life sports hero in my next film, a biography of Muhammad Ali (starring Muhammad Ali) called *The Greatest*, which we made in 1976. I played his loyal manager, Angelo Dundee.

Ali was a strange, unpredictable guy at first. At our first meeting, I put my hand out to introduce myself, but I never got the chance. When he saw me coming, he just looked at me and asked, "Is it true that you worked with Randolph Scott?"

I said, "Yes, it's true."

He said, "What kind of a guy was he?"

I said, "He was a hell of a man."

With that he smiled and walked off, never shook my hand, nothing. Too many shots to the head maybe? Who knows. I will say that he was the most natural acting talent I've ever seen.

Tom Gries, the director, was a brilliant young man who tragically dropped dead of a heart attack after finishing this film. Also in the cast were Robert Duvall, Ben Johnson, James Earl Jones, and John Marley, who a couple of years earlier woke up in bed with a horse's head next to him in *The Godfather*. (I tested for the part of Don Corleone, by the way. So did Burt Lancaster. Neither of us had a shot, really. Francis Ford Coppola wanted Brando—despite the fact that he was considered box-office poison at the time—and fought the studio until he got him.)

Ali had his entourage with him, and people taking pictures, and sometimes he wouldn't come to work until 11:00 in the morning because he didn't feel like getting up. He was the star, so that was that.

We got to know and respect each other as time went on. I had a scene to do with him where he was lying in the hospital after his jaw had been broken in a fight. I called up Angelo Dundee and asked him, "Angelo, how did you react when you were over at the hospital? It says here that you were crying."

He said, "Yes, I was."

I said, "That's all I want to know." So as we got into the scene I cried. We finished the scene and no sooner had we heard "Cut" than Ali asked me, "How did you do that?" He wanted to know how to cry on cue.

I touched my chest and said, "Right from here, from your heart."

He liked that. He even managed to master it. When Ali set his mind to something, he could not be beaten. I must say that we grew to love each other so much that when we parted at the end of the picture, I was crying and he was, too.

That part was real.

I've seen him a few times since, and he always shakes my hand. It's terrible to see him with the affliction he has now, Parkinson's disease. When he was first diagnosed in 1984, pundits said he didn't have long to live. Well, nearly a quarter of a century later, he's still here.

As I said, when Ali sets his mind to something . . .

 ## Crossed Swords (1977)

I'd do pretty much anything for director Richard Fleischer, especially when it plays to his lighthearted side. He was a pretty funny guy. He came by it naturally: his father was Max Fleischer, Disney's chief rival and the man behind the Betty Boop and Popeye cartoons, along with his brother, Dave.

Richard's natural storytelling talents were perfect for this movie, yet another film version of Mark Twain's *The Prince and the Pauper* with an all-star cast that included Rex Harrison, Oliver Reed, Charlton Heston, George C. Scott, and my old friend Raquel Welch. I played John Canty, the gruff, SOB dad of the pauper.

There was one scene where we had a pile of horseshit on the set, which was brought in for authenticity. It was actually easier and, as you can imagine, less expensive to get than fake shit. We were rehearsing nearby when Dick said he wanted me to jump in there to hide.

I looked at him and said, "You mean I got to take a dive into that dung?"

Dick said, "I think that'll work for the scene, don't you?"

I said, "I guess."

Dick said, "Well, let's try it."

I said, "Thanks a lot, Richard," and I would've done it, too. I may be stupid, but I'm a professional.

Right before I jumped, he cracked up and told me to stop, that he'd only been kidding.

I was too relieved to laugh.

Something else that sticks with me was seeing Chuck Heston in full regalia for Henry VIII. Now Chuck's a big guy, six-foot-four, and he made an imposing king. I wondered how accurately this reflected the real king, who was one of the most powerful leaders in history. I know Chuck did a lot of research for his parts, so I went over to ask.

Chuck admitted, "We took some liberties."

"Ah," I thought.

He said, "The real Henry was actually taller than I am."

Chapter 34

Sam Peckinpah Again . . . and Beyond

The last thing Sam Peckinpah had said to me was that I should go fuck myself. So did I want to work with him again?

You bet your life!

It was 1978 and Sam was winding down by this time. The years of boozing and fighting the Hollywood system had taken their toll. He would make one more picture, *The Osterman Weekend*, in 1983 before his untimely death in 1984. Helluva director, but he drove producers and studio executives crazy, always going way beyond schedule and over budget on his films.

I think actors, too, were starting to drive him a little crazy. During the first script reading for *Convoy*, everybody had their own ideas and wanted things changed. That's not unusual; it's one of the reason everyone sits down for these readings.

I'm not sure Sam was listening. I know he didn't change a thing. He knew enough about actors and film to know that as we started shooting, a lot of what we wanted would come out naturally in the performances. He didn't want to be bothered about it until then.

He also couldn't be bothered by schedules.

We had a restaurant scene that was supposed to take a week to film.

It ended up taking four times longer. Finally, the producers went to Sam and said, "What are you doing?"

He looked at them and said, "I don't like anybody looking over my shoulder."

The producers left, but not before telling Sam to move things along or they'd have him replaced. They would have, too. On an earlier picture, *Major Dundee*, they were going to shut the production down until Chuck Heston agreed to return his entire salary to let Sam finish the picture.

I'm not sure I would've done it. (Chuck later told me with a laugh that he wouldn't do it again, either.)

During the filming of *Convoy*, I met Steve McQueen, who was married to costar Ali MacGraw at the time. He came to the location one day while my stand-in Bobby Herron and I were all alone on the set. We were waiting for someone to come along and give us a ride back to the hotel.

Steve asked, "Where's my wife?"

We said, "She's gone ahead to the next location somewhere."

Steve nodded and stood there smoking away. It was marijuana. He made no bones about it.

He said, "Listen, it's getting late. You want me to take you back?"

I said, "Sure." So Bobby and I got into his car. Steve was still smoking and now he was drinking beer at the same time. He had three of these beautiful cowboy hats in the back and he was throwing the empty beer bottles back there with the hats. He was going like a son of a bitch, a hundred miles an hour at least. I know he raced cars professionally, but I was still scared shitless. Bobby sank low in the seat, as scared as I was. We got to the hotel and accepted Steve's invitation to have a beer or three. We left Steve at the bar, where he was just getting his second wind.

I went upstairs and collapsed. The next day Bobby said, "Talk about a ride. I felt like we were in *Bullitt*."

Steve McQueen was a fine actor. You could tell on the screen that he worked the same way I did, with his heart, but also with his head. What this means is, you have to have the scene all prepared and figured out before you let your emotions loose. You've seen how I wrestle with that. So did he, usually carrying the entire picture on his shoulder. Watch him saying nothing on-screen some time. I swear, just watching him think is an exercise in acting!

Ali MacGraw had to have things explained to her a number of times because Sam was very particular in what he wanted from her. He never really gave me direction. I don't know why, but he just let me do my own thing.

I'd say, "Is it okay for you?"

He'd answer, "If it isn't I'll tell you." I'm not kidding: that was it. Once, I had to do this scene in a police cruiser. Before we shot it, I went to Sam to get a few instructions .

He said, "What the fuck do you want?"

I said, "I just want to ask you something about what you want me to do."

"What I want," he said, "is for you to Christ's sake go out there and do the scene."

When Kris Kristofferson saw *Convoy* at the opening, he said to me, "Y'know, I don't remember being in this picture."

He was under the weather most of the time, if you catch my drift. But he had enough charm and sincerity to pull it off. Speaking of which, Sam missed a few days, too, for the same reason. While he was recuperating, actor James Coburn came in and did a little directing work. It was an area he wanted to explore a little more and this was a good opportunity to do it.

It was a pretty good film and was received very well by the public, especially by the truckers. You know, when you can build a fan base like that you know you're going to do okay. And if they like the work you did in it, they'll come back to see you again. I've been really lucky to have accrued a lot of goodwill like that throughout my career.

Incidentally, I'm pretty sure the last thing Sam said to me on the picture was that I should go fuck myself. The man was nothing if not consistent.

The Double McGuffin

I went from working for Sam Peckinpah, a man known for blood and guts, to working for Joe Camp, the director best known for *Benji*.

The Double McGuffin was about some schoolkids who find a briefcase full of money. When they go back to get it, they find a dead body in its place. We had some football players there. Lyle Alzado, who died early in life, God bless him. Rod Browning, Dion Pride, a bunch of great guys. George Kennedy was a police chief and Elke Sommer was a prime minister who was a target for assassins. I was a bad guy.

Joe Camp was very intense; we would do the same scene over and over again.

I'd say, "Joe, what is it that we're doing wrong? Anything we can do to help you?"

He'd say, "No, no, just go ahead."

He was just so concerned about getting it right.

You wouldn't think that you could blank on something in which you invest a couple of months, but that's all I recall about this one.

All Quiet on the Western Front (1979)

Sometimes, despite what Thomas Wolfe said, you *can* go home again.

In 1979 I did a TV remake of the classic film (and Erich Maria Remarque novel) about World War I. It was directed by my old friend Delbert Mann, who had directed me in *Marty*. It was a Hallmark Hall of Fame production—the same group for whom I did my Golden Globe–nominated *A Grandpa for Christmas* in 2007—and we had Richard Thomas, Patricia Neal, Ian Holm, and Donald Pleasence, among many other screen treasures.

We went to Czechoslovakia, which was still under Russian occupation, and shot at a little town called Im. The Russians had pushed all the people out of Im in order to get at the coal underneath. It was a perfect place to shoot because we needed explosives and we needed a blighted landscape where we could use them. This poor town had both.

It was truly disturbing to see these old people come down during the day while we were shooting. They'd look at all these lovely cobblestone streets and their beautiful opera house and churches that were being leveled because the Russians needed coal. You could see the longing in their expressions, remembering how things used to be.

The food was absolutely atrocious. Norman Rosemont, the producer, came to the location and wanted to know what the devil was going on., why the food was so bad. He made some calls and two days later we had people from Spain flown in to cook for us. Not that they always had the raw materials they needed. A few of us borrowed a car and went to Prague on a Sunday morning. We went in a store and asked for a can of beans. There were no beans. They just had empty cans they used for display. The poverty and sadness were terrible. Physically and emotionally, it was a very hard shoot.

The stress we all felt was on the screen and it fit the story. *All Quiet on the Western Front* was a remarkable piece of work. Richard Thomas gave the performance of his life as the hero, a soldier named Paul who learns that war is not about glory. I played a veteran named Private Katczinsky, whom Paul has to carry to a hospital without knowing that I'm already dead.

This picture should be required viewing in schools. There may be such things as necessary wars—I think Iraq and Afghanistan are two such wars, because we have to go after the crazies—but there is no such thing as a good war. We need to remember that.

The Black Hole (1979)

Two years after *Star Wars* set the box office on fire, Disney decided to hop onto the science fiction bandwagon. Actually, that's not quite true. They'd done a number of science fiction movies over the years, things like *The Shaggy Dog* and *Moon Pilot*. What they wanted to do was create a big space picture that could spin off toys and T-shirts and sequels.

The Black Hole is pretty much a retelling of another Disney fantasy film, *20,000 Leagues Under the Sea*. It's about a research vessel that finds a missing spaceship commanded by a mysterious scientist on the edge of a black hole. The Captain Nemo–like scientist was played by Maximilian Schell. My fellow crewmates were Anthony Perkins, Robert Forster, Joe Bottoms, Yvette Mimieux, and Tommy McLoughlin. Roddy McDowall and Slim Pickens did voice-overs for a bunch of robots.

The very first question out of the box from the director, Gary Nelson, when I went to see him about making this picture, was "You don't have to answer me right now, but would you take a trip up into the upper atmosphere of the studio if it came to making this picture there?"

What he meant was, since this was set in space, where there's no gravity, would I do the picture on wires? You know, always floating around inside the spaceship.

I went home and talked it over with Tova, who said, without a whole lot of enthusiasm, "It's up to you."

I told Gary I'd do it. I mean, sure wires can break, but that never stopped anyone from playing Peter Pan on stage. And wouldn't that have been exciting?

Unfortunately, it turned out to be cost-prohibitive, so the idea was scrapped. Too bad. The picture could have used something fresh like that.

It was a long shoot because of all the special effects, and the actors really had to concentrate in order to imagine things that weren't going to be added until months later. With all these serious technicians running around, and Disney executives constantly on the set watching how much was spent—a lot—there wasn't a lot of room for jokes.

The Black Hole turned out to be a beautiful-looking, first-class production, but suffered from being too much like *Star Wars* in the robot department. Action wise, it could have used more of what *Star Wars* had. I'm sure Disney thought so, too, since it was a box-office disappointment for them.

 *Chapter 35*

A Couple of Good Friends

One fine day I was approached by a gentleman who said, "How'd you like to do theater in the round?"

I said, "No, thanks. I gave up theater a long time ago."

He said, "But you'd be doing it with Don Rickles in Neil Simon's *The Odd Couple*."

I said what any half-crazy actor would say upon hearing such news: "Okay. Let me think about it."

I've known Don Rickles ever since he first started out at the Slate Brothers nightclub here in Los Angeles. Don even worked me into his act. He was onstage and, as always, he'd pick out people in the audience and say something sassy. In this case, it was some random woman. Don said, "There she is, ladies and gentlemen, the first runner-up in the Ernest Borgnine look-alike contest." I thought he was so funny that after the show I went backstage, where his mother gave me soup.

Etta Rickles would say, "Stand behind my Don, because he's a good boy."

He is, too. As cutting as he can be onstage, he's warm and loving in private.

I decided to take the job. I'd be playing the slob Oscar Madison, and he'd be the prissy Felix Unger. Perfect. And I figured, what the hell? Don had done a lot of acting, in TV shows like *F-Troop* and *Get Smart* and films like *Kelly's Heroes*. If nothing else, it would be a howl.

We started rehearsing in a room at my house littered with my kids' toys. The first day he didn't know the script at all.

I said, "Listen, you've gotta study these lines."

He said, "What do you mean study? I don't study."

I said, "What do you mean?"

He told me he "kind of" learned lines for movies but did a lot of improvisation. He only had to learn a few lines for any given scene, then go onto the next one. I pointed out the obvious: the stage isn't like that. You need to know the whole play.

I said, "You go home and you learn these lines."

I gave him two pages to rehearse and to come up the next day to do it. He couldn't get it in his head.

I said, "Listen, you've gotta work on these things. It's a show. You're going to perform it in front of people."

He said, "But I don't talk this way."

"You've got to do it the way the author put it down on the page."

He thought about it a little and said, "Okay, I'm going to go home, but I don't think I'm going to last. I don't want to do this."

I said, "Do it or I'll flatten you."

So he went home and started rehearsing. The next day he showed up and we started doing the play. After a couple of weeks we had it down pretty pat.

We went up to San Francisco, where we were set to open. The very first thing he did as he came onstage to check it out was ask, "Where's all the toys?" It knocked me for a loop.

On opening night, everything was moving along nicely. The show opens with us playing poker. Felix wasn't there yet and we were waiting for Don to make his entrance. I know he's going to call me a liar, but this is the truth. He walked onstage like a zombie.

He didn't know where the hell he was going or what he was doing.

He started coming straight across that round stage, instead of coming to the table. I thought, "Oh God, I know it's wrong."

I tried to cover for him by going over and saying, "Hey, what's the matter, Felix?"

It was like the bell sounding for a fighter. He was suddenly back in the game, and he gave the goddamndest performance that I've ever seen in my life. He just came across like a million bucks.

Bob Aldrich came to see the show and said, "Jesus, I fell down on both knees. You are the funniest guys I've ever seen in my life!"

But we didn't play it for fun. I have since seen it with so-called comics that tried and fell flat on their faces because the show wasn't written that way. The comedy comes from the characterizations and the situation—you have to play it as seriously as you would Shakespeare. Otherwise, it just doesn't work.

Neil Simon went in to see Don Rickles after he saw the play. He didn't come in to see me because I was busy with something or other, but I wish he had. I sure would have liked to talk to him. Anyway, he said to Don, "If you ever repeat what I'm about to tell you, I'll deny it. But you two are the first guys that ever did this show the way I had it written."

I'll never forget the comment that Don Rickles made about me when he was interviewed later in his room. Asked if I were good to work with, he answered: "Yes, and if anybody ever says a bad word about that Guinea bastard, I'll kill 'em."

Every time that I have appeared somewhere with him or at his shows he has never spoken my name except with grace and gratitude. He's just one of the most marvelous guys I've ever known in my life. I appreciate it. I want Don to know it, too. So Don, if you're out there reading this, I love you.

Another friend who is really one of the good guys is Mel Larson. How I met Mel was just one of those things. A friend of ours by the name of C. V. Wood was married to Joanne Dru, who starred in *She*

Wore a Yellow Ribbon and many other pictures. They were a great couple. I made a terrible picture with Joanne in 1980, something called *Super Fuzz,* about a cop who gets superpowers after being exposed to radiation. I played his police mentor and Joanne was the wicked Rosy Labouche. It was yesterday's soup warmed over, and not very good soup to start.

Anyway, C.V. came up to me one day and said, "We'd like to have you come up as a judge in a chili contest."

I said, "What the hell is that?"

"Well, you're a good cook. You just come up to where we're having this thing and judge the chili."

I said, "Okay, fine."

He said, "I'll have you picked up at the airport and fly you out."

I went to the airport and in comes this helicopter. Mel Larson is the pilot.

"Hello, how are you?" he asked. "Would you like to sit up front with me?"

I said, "Sure."

The first thing you know we're going along, talking away, getting to know each other. After the chili contest, he brought us back.

That was it until one day a few weeks later, my old buddy George Lindsey—Goober on *The Andy Griffith Show*—said, "Listen, you remember that pilot who flew you to the chili cook-off?"

I said, "Yeah, nice guy. What about him?"

He said, "He's having a birthday and he'd like us to come to Vegas to help celebrate."

That sounded like fun, so off we went.

I had only met Mel that one day, but I discovered that in addition to being a pilot he was one of the executive heads of the Las Vegas casino Circus Circus. We went to Vegas and met him, all togged out in a pink tuxedo. We thought that was a little nutty, but it turned out to be a lot of fun.

Mel and I became good friends from that, which was why he called me up one day and said, "Hey, how'd you like to go cross-country with me, take a helicopter all the way from here to Abingdon, Virginia?"

I said, "I'll go with you on one condition."

He said, "Name it."

I said, "That we buzz the Barter Theatre."

He said, "You got it."

We left and, once airborne, we found Superhighway 40 and simply followed it clean across the country. We landed in all kinds of places. We were going to go down through to New Orleans to visit a friend of his. But it was rainy and foggy and we didn't get too far. By Tennessee he decided, "We better put down." So—I kid you not—we landed by one of those $6.00-a-day motels.

Everybody came running out because they'd never seen a helicopter up close before. Mel checked the weather forecast and it didn't look good, so we stayed there till it lifted, our chopper parked in the lot. Not too many helicopters landed here, evidently. It was like people from outer space had arrived. And when they saw me, people said, "Oh my God, it's Ernest Borgnine!"

The manager was from India. He said to me, "You are a most valued person in India. We love your work, we've loved you for many years. You have a great name over there."

That made me feel pretty good. I could only guess at what Ethel Merman would have done had she heard that.

He gave us two rooms, one for Mel and one for me and we promptly fell asleep. After you've been riding in a helicopter, the silence of even a cheap hotel room is intoxicating. Also, we had imbibed a little bit the night before and we really needed to sleep.

When we woke up it was still miserable out. We weren't going anywhere. The staff took us to lunch and then lent us an automobile so I could buy dry shoes. My feet were getting soaked from the rain. We went into a Wal-Mart. It was close to Christmastime and there was a

Santa Claus there. I said to Mel, "Watch this. I'll go sit on Santa's knee." I went over and sat down. He couldn't see my face clearly because of the whiskers and the fact that I leaned pretty close so none of the kids could hear. I said, "Listen, Santa, I'd like to have a blonde."

He said, without missing a beat, "So would I."

I cracked up. Still laughing, I got myself a pair of shoes and off we went.

After we got home, I went with Mel Larson to his Circus Circus office on Christmas morning. He had to check some work. The telephone rang and it was this man who had been Santa Claus in Tennessee. He had gotten the number from the people at the motel.

He said, "I've got to speak to Ernest Borgnine. I'm the guy that played Santa Claus."

Mel said, "Oh, yes. As a matter of fact he's standing right here."

He gave me the telephone and the guy said, "Do you remember sitting on my lap when I was playing Santa Claus?"

I said, "Uh-huh."

He said "Well, I've got a question to ask you."

"Go ahead and ask."

He said, "I didn't know who you were when you were here. Would you mind very much if they take my picture while I'm talking to you on the phone?"

Oh yeah. Before coming home, we did buzz the Barter Theatre—not during a show, of course—and everybody came out to look. Once we landed, I introduced Mel to the company. I've got to say, I felt like someone had stripped away thirty-plus years. As I looked at the place I remembered what it felt like to be a kid again, scared and a little lost and wondering how the hell things were going to work out.

They turned out okay.

Jimmy Durante and his wife, Marge, were great friends of mine. We used to celebrate New Year's Eve together, and he'd play the piano for us.

As Jimmy got on in years, he pretty much stayed away from the piano. In fact, he'd just sit and not say too much at all. One day, I was looking at the Sunday paper and it showed a marching band in the valley that went around playing for different events. I said, "What a great thing it would be to have a band come over and serenade Jimmy Durante on his birthday."

I called up the band and the leader naturally answered, "Yes, who's calling?"

I said, "This is Ernest Borgnine calling. I'd like to arrange for the band to play."

"Oh, come on, this isn't Ernest Borgnine."

I said, "I'm not kidding."

He said, "Give me your number and I'll call you back." So I gave him the number and he called me back. "Is this really Ernest Borgnine?"

I said, "Yes. Next week is Jimmy Durante's birthday party. I'd like for you and your band to come marching in and really give him a surprise."

On his birthday, two big buses rolled into Beverly Hills to Jimmy's house. Immediately the police were all up in arms saying, "What's going on here?" They thought it was going to be a protest.

I arrived at just about the same time as the Beverly Hills P.D. and said, "It's Jimmy Durante's birthday and this band is going to serenade him."

Talk about an attitude change. The cops couldn't do enough for us. We went marching through Beverly Hills to his home, then surrounded the home and played a serenade for Jimmy. He got so excited that he threw open the door, went over to the piano, and started playing "Inka Dinka Do." He came out of his slump and, for that short hour or two, he was the happiest man in the world. I don't have to tell you how happy it made me to see how much he was enjoying it.

When he passed away in January of 1980, and they were lowering the casket into the ground, I said to Marge, "Would you mind very much if I say something?"

She said, "No, not at all."

I said, through tears, my voice choking, "All right, folks. Let's hear it one more time for Jimmy Durante."

Everybody started to applaud.

Chapter 36

Back to Work

When Time Ran Out (1980)

It did, sort of, for Irwin Allen

In 1980, following the failure of a couple of big films—*The Swarm* and *Beyond the Poseidon Adventure*—Irwin tried for the gold once again with another huge disaster epic about a volcano. He had Paul Newman in the lead, with Jacqueline Bisset, William Holden, Red Buttons, and a bunch of others, including me. My character is a cop out to nab Red Buttons, who's a crook.

Paul Newman, as I understand, did not want to make this movie. He was still under contract to Irwin Allen since costarring in *The Towering Inferno,* so he had to make it, but he wasn't very amiable. Irwin's plan had been to do a sequel to *The Towering Inferno* with Paul as the star, but it never came about after the sequel to *The Poseidon Adventure* flopped. In the few times I saw him after we made the picture, Paul was never one of the more outgoing guys you'd want to meet. He's another of the shy ones I was talking about.

Part of the problem with this picture was that Irwin didn't have enough money to make it. We were on location in Hawaii, which was nice but very costly. The stars were expensive. That meant cutting corners on the sets and the all-important special effects, which were down-right cheesy.

The film was a failure and was Irwin's last theatrical picture. He made a handful of TV movies after that, but he never recaptured that two-picture moment of glory he enjoyed in the early 1970s, or on TV in the 1960s. He died in 1991 at the age of seventy-five of a heart attack. I was sad, but not surprised.

The industry he'd loved and given so much to had broken his heart. Knowing Irwin, though, he wouldn't have had it any other way. He was a master showman, the kind Hollywood doesn't build anymore.

 ### *Escape from New York (1981)*

One day in late 1980 I got a call from John Carpenter.

John had a big youth following thanks to the horror movie he'd made three years earlier, *Halloween. Escape from New York* is a futuristic story in which Manhattan island is a maximum-security prison and breaking out is impossible. When the President of the United States is taken prisoner after a plane crash, Kurt Russell is sent to rescue him.

I received the script from John, who said, "I'd love to have you play the cabby in this picture." I read it and I admit I couldn't make head or tail out of it. I was one of the convicts imprisoned there, an old-time New York taxi driver. I played a hack in *The Catered Affair,* so I figured it wouldn't be much of a stretch.

I had a meeting with John Carpenter and he said, "I want you to play the cabby."

I said "I don't want to play the cabby. I want to play the warden."

He said, "I've already got the warden cast." He'd given the part to Lee Van Cleef. "I wrote the cabby especially for you."

I said, "I can do this standing on my head."

"I know you can."

We shot in St. Louis because the city had had a really devastating fire in one section of town and it was perfect for the kind of destroyed landscape Carpenter wanted. Kurt Russell was fantastic as always as the one-eyed Snake Plissken who is sent to rescue the President. When I saw Kurt a couple of years later, he had just moved with his girl-friend Goldie Hawn and their kids to a huge ranch outside of Aspen. Hunting and riding and living the life of the cowboy and having a burger with the locals at a greasy diner was something that Kurt said had always appealed to him.

When filming on *Escape from New York* was finished, we went to see the picture at the Screen Actors Guild and don't you know that everybody sat on their hands until it came to when I get killed. The au-dience went, *"Awww."* They hated to see me die—my cabby is the one lovable character in the picture. I thought it was a heck of a tribute.

I'll say this about John Carpenter. He was right when he said, "It's the best thing I could do for you." I thank him very much because he was a good director and *Escape from New York* was a good popcorn movie that introduced me to a new generation of moviegoers

I'm Going to Make You an Offer You Can't Refuse

One day when we are in St. Louis, on location for *Escape from New York*, I was watching television while waiting to be called to the set. I saw a show about the human brain and how little we actually use of it. About 10 percent, they said. Now, at this time I was worried silly about doing this one-man show that Sam Gallu had written for me. It was a Mafia piece called *I'm Going to Make You an Offer You Can't Refuse*, a dissertation on the United States as seen through the eyes of a capo Mafioso, and I was worried stiff. I'd promised to do a read-ing—"off book," which means without the script—in a few weeks. Problem was, the lines weren't sticking in my head. Maybe Don Rick-les had put a curse on me or something. More likely, I was feeling the long hours on the last two shoots plus my sixty-four years.

The program about the brain happened to mention hypnotism. I wondered if it would be possible for me to find a hypnotist to put me under and order me to get my lines into my head. That may sound silly, but I was desperate. And tired. That's a dangerous combination. I called Tova back in L.A. and asked her to see if she could find someone. Tova's a great gal—she didn't think I was crazy. She's pretty open-minded. She has to be, being married to an actor.

She found a hypnotist, and when I came home I went to see him. The first thing he asked was, "Do you want to know everything that goes on?"

I said, "Of course."

He explained, "Not everyone does. Some people have to go really deep to remember events from their past. They rely on me to take notes."

I didn't want anyone I didn't know putting me to sleep, so I told him to keep me close to the surface.

He said okay and, leaning close, he said in a very soothing voice, "Watch that clock up on the wall, the way the pendulum is swinging back and forth."

I did. It was like out of some cornball horror movie. But I watched and my mind started to wander here and there. He later explained that was the point: to uproot you from the "now" and let your mind float freely. That is what makes it particularly responsive to the hypnotist's voice and open to suggestion. After a minute or two or three—it could have been a half hour, I was kind of daydreaming—he said, "When I say count to five you will be under."

I said, "Sure I will, yep."

So he said, "One, two, three, four, five," and I was supposed to be under.

I didn't feel any different, but I continued to watch the clock. We talked about my family, my this, my that and everything else—more of that freeing-my-brain-from-restraints, I later learned—and there was a point when I decided to uncross my legs, which I'd crossed at the ankles. I tried but I could not move them. I realized that, sure enough, nothing was working except my brain and my answering him. Eventually he got around to telling me to let go of my fear of the one-man show and learn the lines.

When I got home, I opened the script and believe it or not, within a half hour I had thirty-seven pages of dialogue in my head. Within a week, I gave a performance in front of people in my home.

I went out on the road for about three months with the show, but it was badly promoted, though people who came liked it very much. Still, I didn't come away from the experience empty-handed.

Years later, when I was doing the TV show *Airwolf*, my costar David Carradine came up to me looking really distracted.

I said, "Something bothering you?"

He said, "Oh God, I've got this one-man show to do and I'm scared spitless."

I said, "I know exactly what you're talking about and also what to do."

"You do?"

I said, "Go see this hypnotist I know."

He went to see the guy. When I saw Dave later, he said, "It was absolutely incredible."

We never put the mob show on for the public, though I did get to put the hypnotism to good use two years later. My publicist, Harry Flynn, kept asking me if I would like to do a one-man show called *Hoover*, about J. Edgar Hoover, the onetime head of the FBI.

I kept putting him off, because Hoover was not a very likable guy. And that's tough to sustain onstage, alone, for ninety minutes.

But he kept after me and kept after and I finally agreed to do it down in Florida. Later that year we did a version of it for TV called *Blood Feud*, but with a full cast that included Robert Blake, who snagged an Emmy nomination as Jimmy Hoffa. But back to the stage.

The hypnotism obviously "stuck" because I had no trouble learning the script, though they supplied me with big offstage cue cards that I could read from if I got into trouble. It was almost like a live television show.

Doing research for the play and then the movie, trying to find a human side to Hoover, I found out that he was an honest person. Whatever his methods—and some of them weren't very nice—he believed he was protecting America. This country meant everything to him. I could relate to that. People said he was a cross dresser and a homosexual because he had a good male friend. But you know, when you're in a position of power you'll always find jealous people saying things that aren't true. I found out that he was quite a gentleman and a good friend of actress Dorothy Lamour. He lived with her for years and then later on when she passed away he lived by himself. When I mentioned that to someone, he cracked, "Yeah, maybe he wanted to borrow her sarongs." Even if it *was* true, so what?

See what I mean? When you're in the public eye, you become a target. All too often jokes that are made about you, like the gossip written about celebrities, are taken as gospel, they get passed around. Most of it isn't true.

Deadly Blessing (1981)

Crazy thing about Hollywood. When you're in a hit, you become typecast in that genre, like Chuck Heston in biblical epics and Clint Eastwood in westerns. But I'd done a successful western, a successful disaster picture, a successful horror picture, and an example of just about every other genre under the sun. So I was accepted by audiences in many genres and was brought in as a familiar face—"insurance," they called it—to help make sure those audiences turned up.

Thanks to *Willard* and *The Devil's Rain*, I was "insurance" for horror pictures—that is why I was asked to do this one.

Wes Craven had become "the" horror guy, having directed *A Nightmare on Elm Street* and, later, *Scream*. I found him to be a laid-back but articulate and knowledgeable director. Later I found out he had started as a crewman in porn flicks. Maybe that explains why nothing rattled him.

Deadly Blessing is set in Amish country at a local farm, where a woman's husband is mysteriously killed by his own tractor. My character is the evil Isaiah Schmidt, the family patriarch, who is protecting a nasty old secret.

It was a pretty routine shoot, except for the time when Wes tried to persuade Sharon Stone to film a scene with a very large spider. Sharon wanted the spider's pincers removed before she agreed to do the scene. Since someone from the ASPCA might be reading, let's just skip what happened next. I'll tell you this: no one knew in 1981 that she'd become a big star.

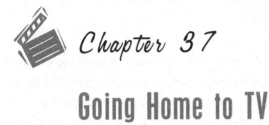

Chapter 37

Going Home to TV

In 1982 I was invited to do a two-part episode of *The Love Boat* playing the husband of Shelley Winters. After fifty years they decide to get a divorce. The children had grown up and their feelings for each other had faded. But I ended up singing love songs to her in Italian on a gondola in the Grand Canal in Venice and we rediscovered our love.

This is a case of life not imitating art.

It was the first time I'd worked with Shelley since *The Poseidon Adventure* ten years earlier. There were choppy seas on *The Love Boat*.

When we were on location it was fine. When we returned to the studio in Los Angeles it got to the point where I just couldn't stomach her anymore. She was the damnedest woman you've ever seen in your life.

She'd come in after being out half the night, and say, "Oh, Ernie, I feel terrible. Could you help me with my lines?"

I knew my lines and, like most actors, knew the gist of what the other person had to say, so I helped her. But I would have to go over it again and again. Of course, when she came to the set the stuff was fresh in her memory and I'd forgotten my lines.

Exasperating is a good word for her. She said at one point, "You better be nice to me or I won't put you in my autobiography," which she was writing at the time.

I said, "Thank God."

Before we get to one of my most disappointing work experiences, there's a sort of prelude story. Ages before, in 1960, Sam Gallu, the author of *I'm Going to Make You an Offer You Can't Refuse*, had written a documentary about the Blue Angels. They're the navy's famous aerobatic team, made up of some of the best pilots on earth. He asked me to do the narration, and it was an honor to do so. After that, we went to meet the team in Pensacola, Florida. Of course, we all went out and got blasted.

The next morning these guys got up and flew like crazy while I watched with a blazing headache. The Blue Angels made me an honorary skipper and I've been their skipper ever since. It's been a tremendous pleasure to watch these young pilots—who are drinking a lot less, these days—who are part of the team for two years, then they move on to make room for the boys coming up.

I'll never forget my first trip on one of the planes. It was about five years later. I came down from Alabama where I was making a picture. No sooner had I got there than they welcomed me and put me right into a flight suit.

"Come on," they said. "We're going to give you a ride."

As soon as I was belted in, the pilot, Lieutenant Mike Nord, said to me, "Mr. Borgnine, we're going to go straight down the runway."

"Okay."

"Then we're gonna go straight up into the air."

We did. We went up and my neck hit my backbone and seemed to travel down to my butt. I couldn't move my head for a month. He told me to turn so I could see Pensacola. Well, I couldn't turn my head at all because of the Gs we were pulling.

While we were up there, he called one of the aircraft carriers that were having maneuvers out in the Gulf, and said, "Listen, I got a VIP aboard, can we make a pass?"

They wanted to know who it was and he told them. They said, "McHale? Give us ten minutes."

So we went along the coast. He knew a nude beach where all the naked ladies were. Talk about torture. I still couldn't turn my head, I couldn't see for nothing.

But there was one thing I could see. The pilot made sure of that. We made a pass by the ship and I'll never forget this as long as I live. They had called all hands on deck to salute Ernest Borgnine, Lieutenant Commander McHale. I got the biggest lump in my throat you could imagine.

What a wonderful honor.

I mention this now because my next TV project was about fliers. Only it turned out not to be such an honor or very much fun.

In 1984, Don Bellisario offered me a part in a pilot he was doing called *Airwolf*, about the crew of a hi-tech helicopter. I was thinking that audiences would have a great time if we could capture some of that "right stuff" Blue Angels spirit I had experienced.

I'll never forget the first day of shooting. We watched the pilot, Tommy Jones, take our customized helicopter through an amazing series of maneuvers, right there at the studio. He went behind a building and backed it out again and ran it around like an automobile. I couldn't believe my eyes.

We got along fine for the first few weeks. Then everything started to dribble away. People were showing up late and they weren't really that anxious to make the thing. It lasted for three seasons, from 1984 to 1986, and it was a chore.

At the beginning, our leading man, Jan-Michael Vincent, was absolutely sensational. I mean, he'd look at a piece of script, one glance, and say, "Okay, let's go." He had a photographic memory.

I said, "My God, how can you do that?"

He'd just shrug. Some people got it and some people—like me— have to get hypnotized.

Unfortunately, Jan-Michael was having personal problems that infected the set and brought everyone down. There was drinking, altercations, a whole lot of stuff that really distracted him. After *Airwolf* limped to its finish, the poor guy's luck got worse. In 1996 he broke his neck in a car accident and messed up his voice, permanently. He also served jail time for probation violations. Last I heard he was living in Mississippi, where he has a horse ranch. I hope he's happy.

My next TV job was another disappointment: a sequel to *The Dirty Dozen* called *The Dirty Dozen: The Next Mission.* Lee Marvin returned, looking tired and unhappy. He had been the center of a huge legal mess, a historic palimony suit brought by his live-in lady, Michelle Triola. It had taken everything out of him, and he'd taken to drinking heavily. He only made one more movie, *Delta Force,* after this one, before dying of a heart attack in 1987 at the age of sixty-three. We did our work, reprised our roles in this uninspired clambake, and got the hell out of there. I can't remember a more bittersweet experience on a picture.

Lee, by the way, was Steven Spielberg's first choice for the role of Quint in *Jaws.* Lee thanked him, but replied that he'd rather go fishing. As great as Robert Shaw was in the picture, I still wonder how *Jaws* might have turned out with Lee as the salty old shark hunter.

I still miss the hell out of him.

Next up was a TV version of *Alice in Wonderland* for Irwin Allen. It was great to see him again, in what proved to be his last hit and his second-to-last film. As usual, he'd assembled quite a cast: Red Buttons, Sammy Davis, Jr., Donald O'Connor, Telly Savalas, Shelley Winters (whom I avoided), Imogene Coca and Sid Caesar, Ringo Starr—just a slew of great names. I ended up locked in a lion suit with a big heavy head. When they took that thing off between shots I was redder than a cooked lobster.

One time I practically fainted inside that thing. They wanted to take me to the hospital.

I said, "I don't need a hospital. All I need is fresh air." It was terrible.

Irwin was very concerned and kept making sure I was okay. It was a case of déjà vu for us. During *The Poseidon Adventure,* there was a scene where I was dragging Gene Hackman from the water. I pulled so hard that I actually threw my back out. I couldn't straighten up, so they took me to the hospital and they took X-rays. Irwin Allen came by, wringing his hands and saying, "Oh my God, we're lost."

I said, "Don't worry about it. It's just a slipped disc."

They put one of those corsets on me and I wore it for about a half hour. I couldn't breathe, so I said, "To hell with this," and pulled it off and went back to work. I was fine, though I didn't pull anyone else from the drink.

Luckily, I only had to stay in the lion suit for two days. Frankly, out there in the hot sun, I don't know how lions do it!

 *Chapter 38*

And Now for Some Things Completely Different

I've owned a pair of forty-foot bus motor homes—they're called RVs now. The first one I didn't like too well because the toilet seat was a little small for my big rump, so when I went up to Oregon on a shoot, I took my trailer. I figured someone up there could remodel it for me. I went to a place in Cottage Grove, Oregon, where they suggested that instead of spending a lot of money to fix it, I take a look at their RVs. So I went in one and the first thing I saw was all the leather inside. It was decorated in a western motif. That appealed to me. The second thing I noticed was the nice, big toilet just to sit on and enjoy. That's what it's all about.

I said, "How much?"

Long story short: I probably should have ripped out the toilet of my old bus. This one cost me. But they gave me a good trade-in and I had a new motor home.

As I was leaving, I spotted a man who was pacing up and down in the motor home lot. He looked like a decent sort so I pulled over and said, "What's the matter?"

He said, "I'm waiting for my rig."

I said, "Have you had lunch?"

He said, "No."

I said, "Then let's go."

We had lunch, came back, and we've been buddies ever since. His name is Hugo Hansen and since then we've gone from coast to coast and up and down and across into Canada. We even went to Alaska together. It's a magnificent way to see our great country.

One day in 1997, a filmmaker from Washington, D.C., named Jeff Krulik called and said, "Listen, I'd like to do a documentary on you."

At first I wasn't interested, but the fellow kept insisting.

Finally, I said, "Okay, come on, we'll do it."

My son Cris, Hugo, and I started out from Milwaukee after I had done one of the shows there for the Great Circus Parade. Jeff followed us for about three days. He taped me visiting here and there, stopping off for ice cream, and talking to people in towns as we passed through. We even got lost in a cornfield. People are still writing to me about the show called *Ernest Borgnine: On the Bus.* They thought it was a great way to see the U.S., and more important, they loved seeing it through my eyes, hearing me explain what I was seeing and feeling. We planned to do a whole series on my journeys, but it never panned out. It made my early eighties very exciting, I can tell you.

That same year I got a call from a very nice young man named Brad Hall, the producer of an NBC sitcom called *The Single Guy.* He asked if I'd come down to his office and say hello. When you're an elder statesman in the business like I've become, you frequently get calls like that. Since you never know where they lead, I said sure. I took my publicity man, Harry Flynn, and we went to meet Brad Hall.

The receptionist said, "Well, what's your name?"

I told her. She looked about twelve years old and obviously she had no idea who I was. So we waited and we waited. It must have been about a half hour and finally the girl said, "They're busy, but they'll be here right away."

I finally said, "The hell with it, I won't wait any longer."

About an hour later I got a telephone call—it was Brad Hall, and he sounded very stressed out.

"Mr. Borgnine, you've got to forgive us, but we were so busy with something else and we just couldn't get to you. But listen, you've got the part, don't worry."

I said, "Okay."

I didn't know I'd been there *for* a part, but that's how it is now in Hollywood. When they say they want to "see" you or "meet" you, it means they want you for something other than to say hello.

They wanted me to play a doorman on *The Single Guy*, and I did.

The first time I reported in, everybody was a little bit in awe. Here I was, an Academy Award winner, playing a doorman. I showed them that no matter how good you were before, it's how good are you now that counts. My feeling is, you don't rest on your laurels, you keep going. You're never too old to keep learning and honing your craft.

The Single Guy had wonderful young actors. The star was Jonathan Silverman, a very talented guy with a fine sense of comic timing. For some reason the network lost interest after forty episodes. But people who watched it still tell me how much they enjoyed it.

Another benefit from being an elder statesman is that people who grew up watching me in pictures like *The Wild Bunch, The Poseidon Adventure,* and *Escape from New York* are now in positions of power. They're the young Turks running the show.

One day I got a call out of the blue.

"I wonder if we could use Mr. Borgnine's voice in a feature-length cartoon called *All Dogs Go to Heaven?*"

I was very interested. I hadn't done any animation voice-overs and I wanted to try.

I signed on and found a whole new legion of fans. I also discovered that doing voice-overs is almost like stealing money, to put it bluntly. You don't have to memorize anything, there are no costumes or makeup, and usually it's just you in a recording studio with the director. No temperamental costars, no fuss. It's a great way to make a living.

The picture was a success and more recently I've got a steady gig playing Mermaid Man on *SpongeBob SquarePants*.

One day when I was in Washington, D.C., after I gave a speech at the Washington Press Club, I was asked to meet with a group of little Girl Scouts who had sent a lot of cookies and other things to the troops in Iraq. Would I mind taking a picture with them?

I walked over and someone was telling all these kids that I'm a famous movie star.

I asked them, "How many of you have seen my pictures?"

Nobody raised an arm. So I asked, "How many of you have heard of Mermaid Man on *SpongeBob SquarePants*?"

That was all it took. They couldn't get enough pictures and autographs. It was wonderful.

Sometimes people walk up to me and say, "Your face is awfully familiar, but who are you?"

I tell them my name is Ernest Borgnine, and they say, "Yes, but who *are* you?"

I tell them. Big smiles usually follow, along with all kinds of compliments.

A generation ago, they would have known me as McHale. A generation before that, as Fatso Judson or Marty. Now it's Mermaid Man on *SpongeBob SquarePants* that's made me famous to a new generation, or playing myself in voice-over on *The Simpsons*.

Believe me, I'm not complaining.

Chapter 39

More Special Folk

ova and I were shopping one day about 1974 and we decided to have dinner at the Polo Lounge in the Beverly Hills Hotel. In case you don't know, that's the place where Hollywood movers and shakers used to go to be seen and see others. We didn't call it networking in those days, we called it brown-nosing.

The Polo Lounge is a pretty elegant place with good food, and chances are good you'll run into old friends there.

We were just leaving when along came John Wayne with his wife Pilar. We knew each other socially a little, and the two ladies got started talking. I thought, "There goes the afternoon." John and I decided to go into the bar to get a drink. As soon as we had ordered, John said to me, "Ernie, it looks like we've known each other forever. How come we've never worked together?"

I'd had a couple of drinks, maybe too many, and I said, "We've never worked together because you're afraid to work with good actors."

I thought he'd fall down. The minute I said it I bit my tongue, but the Duke just laughed uproariously. He knew I was kidding deep down.

Something about my manner makes a lot of what I say seem good-natured. We talked about the "old days" and mutual friends and how there were fewer and fewer of us as the years passed.

The next time I saw Duke Wayne was when he was being made a 32nd degree Mason at the House of the Temple on Wilshire Boulevard. Boy, could he take a joke and ribbing with the best of 'em.

He took a lot of flak in his later years because of his open patriotism. I never saw that as a bad thing. Remember, there was an ocean of movement in the other direction during Vietnam and after, with guys like Burt Lancaster and Greg Peck playing for the liberals. America needed guys like the Duke and, later, Chuck Heston to balance the scales.

I'm sorry we never worked together. But I'm sorrier that people didn't get to know him for the sweet guy he was.

Bob Mitchum was another actor I really liked on camera and off. I got to work with him in a TV movie called *Jake Spanner, Private Eye* in 1989. I always loved the way he handled himself in front of a camera, natural like Cooper but with a little bit of quiet menace to him. I'd watch him like a hawk on that shoot because, believe me, you can learn so much from watching the real pros.

And stories! He had a million of 'em. We'd do a scene and immediately after they said "Cut, print," he'd start telling great stories about things, like his friendship with Howard Hughes ("he liked me because he never really got to know me"), his time in rehab ("I did it because producers couldn't get insurance on me otherwise") and how he made George C. Scott a superstar by turning down *Patton*. ("That picture needed someone who was willing to fight the tanks and big battles for screen time. I didn't care enough about Patton to do that.")

I'll never forget, we were right in the middle of a scene where I'm chasing him or he's chasing me. Okay—that part I forget. But he had just told me some story or other and, for some reason, we couldn't stop laughing. That was one of the few times in my career I had to take a time-out before being able to continue.

Before Bob passed away, his son called and asked if I would lend my support toward getting him an honorary Oscar for all his great work. I went to the top guy and said, "Please—here's a man who doesn't have long to live. He's got an amazing body of work. Why can't we give him the ultimate gift of an Oscar?"

They turned me down. I didn't know why, but to this day I'm not too happy about it.

If anybody ever deserved some kind of lifetime achievement Oscar, it was Bob Mitchum.

I mentioned my friend George Lindsey back a ways, and I want to say a little more about him. He's a character who came into my life in the 1970s. My marriage to Donna was on the rocks and I needed to get out of the house for a while. One day I took my car and I was so upset, I almost went over a cliff in the Hollywood hills. I needed to calm down, so I went to my gas station at the foot of the hill and said, "Oil, grease it, do something, I'm going to go for a cup of coffee."

While I was having my coffee, in walks this guy.

He said, "Hello, how are you? My name is George Lindsey. I play Goober on *The Andy Griffith Show*."

I knew of him, of course, though we'd never met. We started talking and the first thing you know we were on a golf course. The next thing you know we were out in his car driving around the mountains and talking. By the end of the day, when I went to pick up my car, it was like I had been to a psychiatrist. From that day, whenever George had a problem with his marriage or I did with mine, or if we were down about work or life in general, we'd get together, we'd go out. We'd play golf, we'd have lunch or dinner, we'd shop. We even went out to watch farmers grow parsley. We became really great good buddies.

To this very day I think that George Lindsey is one of the great-est guys in the world. I can't say too much about that old boy and how he used to keep me in stitches talking about his home in Alabama, how he gave up being a science teacher to act, and how—my hand to God—he turned down the part of Mr. Spock on TV's *Star Trek*, the role that made Leonard Nimoy famous. He even convinced me to do a guest appearance on a TV show he was working on at the time, *Hee Haw*, with Roy Clark and Buck Owens and all those *Hee Haw* honeys. I don't get to do as much comedy as I like, so I had a helluva time.

Thanks, buddy. Thanks for everything.

There are two more people I have to tell you about briefly.

Ever since I first enlisted in 1935, the navy's been part of my life. It's afforded me the opportunity to meet some wonderful people. One day, a really close navy friend, Captain Kathy Dugan—the one-time head of the Philadelphia Navy Yard—called me and said, "Listen, would you do me a favor?"

I said, "Anything."

She wanted me to send a pep talk via e-mail to the crew of a cruiser that had been in the Persian Gulf for six months.

I was a little hesitant at first, not sure what to say and less sure that most of the kids would know who I was, but I took the bull by the horns and wrote a long e-mail, one finger at a time, because that's the way I do it. I plugged away and finally sent it off.

Lo and behold, I had a note back in no time at all from Captain Peter Squicciarini. "I have posted your e-mail up on the bulletin board," he said. "The guys are just crazy to meet you."

When they came back to Norfolk, Peter Squicciarini was on the list to be relieved as the skipper of the Cruiser USS *Monterey*. They in-vited me to go to Norfolk for the change-of-command ceremony.

Peter and his crew showed me an incredible time. There I was, over eighty years of age, running up and down and across and over that whole ship. I saw the engine room, the gunnery department, the whole thing from the bridge to the bilge. Believe me, that's one big ship.

But it still wasn't as big as its skipper. On the day that Peter Squicciarini was relieved of his command, I saw it in his eyes: the realization that there would be no more going to sea for him. He loved the ocean, he loved being the skipper of a ship, and his crew loved him.

I knew that feeling and I told him so. Afterward, he said how much it meant for me to say that. My own example reminded him that ending a long career in the navy was just the start of the next phase of his life.

That had nothing to do with me being an actor. It had to do with me being a former navy man. I don't think enough of us realize how, in big ways and small, we have the ability to touch other people.

This would be as good a time as any to suggest, by the way, that you get out and do what you can for our veterans. I was on *The Larry King Show* one night and I started crying while we were talking about the war in Iraq.

I said, "Please, for heaven's sake, if anybody lives next to a hospital, a veteran's hospital or something, take a half hour, take an hour, take two hours, and go down there and visit our veterans. They would love to see you. Bring 'em flowers or something. Just to say hello. Believe me, they're hungry for people to come and see them."

More than that, they deserve our thanks, in person. I've gone many times, around the country, and it's never failed to move them, and me. We owe our freedom and opportunity to them. It's the least all of us can do.

The last guy who needs mentioning here is Bobby Herron. When I first started in pictures, I did all my own stunts. In westerns, they'd say "Get on the horse" and I'd be in the saddle in a minute. If I was in a war picture, they'd say "Stand by that explosion" and I did.

While we were making the 1953 western *The Stranger Wore a Gun*, Bobby Herron came up to me and said, "You know, mister, you're taking the bread out of our mouths."

I said, "What do you mean?"

He said, "When they tell you to jump on the horse, you have the right to use a stuntman for that."

I said, "I thought they'd think I was a scaredy-cat."

He said, "No. They'd think you were smart. When they ask you to do that stuff, they're just trying to get out of paying us."

You may recall how frightened I really was doing the run down the hill with that horse, the one that had Lee Marvin tsk-tsking. I gathered up the reins and said, "Please take them. I am so happy to know this."

What I didn't know about riding horses was in proportion to what Bobby Herron *did* know.

Bobby and I have been together in just about every picture where I needed a horseman or somebody to do a "gag"—a stunt trick—for me. As a matter of fact, he did a stunt in *Convoy* that could've killed him. I played a cop who was supposed to be chasing a truck. The way that the script read, my car was supposed to go off the cliff, right through the middle of a signpost, and into a building full of chickens.

There weren't any instruments in these cars, and the way Bobby was strapped in he couldn't have read them anyway. There was no way of knowing how much velocity he'd achieved. And, honestly, no way to stop, either, since the brakes were mostly disconnected. The whole thing about a stunt car is that it gets stripped down so that parts aren't dislodged in the crash and become projectiles.

When he went through the signpost, he not only went through the top of this house where the chickens came flying out, he landed about two-hundred feet even farther. There was a camera mounted in the car filming him as he did it.

He tore every bit of cartilage off his ribs. Before he passed out, he turned off the motor and the camera. Watching him sail through the air, I thought for sure that he'd killed himself.

Did I mention that these stunt guys are tough? Two weeks later, we were playing golf together.

That's why, when critics say, "*Convoy* was a so-so picture," don't you believe it. Audiences aren't as jaded as critics. And none of them knows just what stuntmen go through to make pictures look real.

 *Chapter 40*

Dedicated to the Ones I Love

I've written about the people who have helped me and impressed me and whose lives intersected with mine only briefly, but made a big impact. As I look back, there are others who played roles large and small in bringing me to this point.

Foremost among these is my right-hand woman, Joyce McConnell.

I stole Joyce from Tova over twenty years ago. She was sitting there at her desk in Tova's business office, where she helped with the skin care merchandise, and I happened to stop by. I was thinking about how distracting it was that I was still answering my own phone, typing my own correspondence—badly, as I've indicated—instead of studying scripts. I felt it was time to change that, so I said, "Do you want to work for me?"

She said, "Okay."

That was that. I guess she felt she'd have more fun in the movies.

So we set up an office in my home and Joyce has been here ever since.

She's more than a secretary. She's a confidante. She takes care of the house while I'm gone on location, if Tova's not around. She's a jack of all trades—handles all my correspondence and computer stuff and protects me from scam artists who try to use my name, fame, and money. She's a very, very good woman, tough when she needs to be. It's been a pleasure to have her with me. She's happily married to her husband Bob, who became a meat cutter after he got out of the marines. He's retired and now plays senior softball. He knocks them out of the park all the time, and takes great pride in it. I'll say, "How'd you hit 'em today?" He'll say, "Nine out of nine." I'll say "Not bad!" God bless Joyce and Bob. I was the best man at their wedding. Ours has been a wonderful association. They're both very special people.

Another person who helps me personally and professionally is Brent Braun. He came up to the house to introduce himself when he was in the FBI's Los Angeles office. He wanted me to speak at a ceremony honoring fallen FBI agents. It was a moving experience, and since then Brent has become a good friend. I call him my hired gun. He's retired from the FBI now and involved in a variety of public-service ventures, which includes looking after my ass when personal security could be a problem and also teaching me how to handle weapons properly on camera. You shouldn't fake that stuff, you know. Not unless you want to hear from a few thousand people who do know what they're doing!

Italians gravitate toward one another and Larry Manetti and I gravitated. We met when I guest-starred in an episode of *Magnum P.I.* in Hawaii. Larry was one of the costars with Tom Selleck—who, for the record, is absolutely the sweetest, gentlest man. The first thing you know, Larry and I were out eating, sampling various Waikiki restaurants, enjoying each other's company. We still do. He brings over meals that he cooks himself.

Larry and I spent one memorable afternoon visiting Frank Sinatra. We went to his summer home on the Pacific Coast. There we were, Frank, Larry, and myself eating spaghetti and talking about old times. No star egos, no checkbook, just three Italians gravitating.

* * *

I met A. C. Lyles while doing *Run For Cover* with Cagney. A. C. was doing the publicity for Paramount on that picture. He and Cagney were friends and shared a suite at the hotel. Later, Cagney made his only directorial effort on a Paramount picture that A.C. produced, *Shortcut to Hell*. A.C.'s been at Paramount for over seventy years— no kidding!—and has been a good friend of mine for over fifty of them. He and his lovely wife Martha are among the most respected couples in Hollywood, true movie nobility!

Alex Cord, on *Airwolf*, has been a real anchor in the shaky times there, willing to do his share and more. He's a wonderful actor and has become quite a noted author as well. He's a horseman of the first water, plays polo, and lives on a beautiful ranch with his wife in Texas. Whenever he comes to town, we get together and talk old times.

I consider myself lucky to have these people in my life. I hope all of you have people like them in yours.

Last but far from least, I want to say how very grateful I am for my three children, Nancee, Sharon, and Cristofer.

Nancee—who, you may recall, was born while I was onstage with Helen Hayes doing *Mrs. McThing* and had Ms. Hayes as godmother— grew up in the midst of a bad divorce. She was always being pushed and pulled. It wasn't the most pleasant thing for a little girl like her, but she made the best of it. Her mother passed away a number of years ago, but today, I must say, my daughter and I are the best of friends.

The same is true of Sharon and her year-younger brother Cristopher. Even after we hadn't had contact for so long, we are very close friends and she has a beautiful family of her own.

Cristofer was my miracle kid. He was a sickly baby, and I remember sitting in an ambulance holding him in my hands, begging him, "Hey, kid, come on, you've got to pull yourself together. We've got to make this thing go, baby."

I'm happy to say that today he's a robust man with two kids of his own.

It wasn't a miracle that it all worked out for us: it took a lot of hard work and forgiving, on their part. But they did it—*we* did it—and have never, ever taken our relationships for granted.

To any parent or child who is reading this book, I want to say, fathers and mothers are just people, which means they make mistakes. Don't hold that against them. Whatever flaws they may have, they created you in a moment of love and are among the few who "knew you when." When they're gone, there won't be anyone to take their place.

 *Chapter 41*

Odds and the End

Parenting and these glorious United States aren't the only soapboxes to which I'm going to subject you, just a little. There's something else I feel quite strongly about, and that's smoking.

I tried smoking when I was a kid, with some of my father's old Italian stogies. I remember my buddy Joey and I were at the top of the hill. By the time we finished those stogies we were down at the bottom. We had rolled down, sicker than dogs. It kind of held me off smoking until I was around eighteen and joined the navy. I saw everybody else smoking cigarettes, so it came kind of naturally.

I was going along smoking mostly Bull Durham in those days. Cigarettes only cost five cents a pack at the navy PX and we didn't realize that it was really an addiction.

Just before I started *McHale's Navy* I was smoking five packs a day. I had become a chain-smoker. My fingertips were brown from the smoke. I would cough from the morning until about midday. It wasn't a problem when I was doing a scene, because I was concentrating on something else. But when I was just by myself I would cough like a madman.

One day I woke up and my voice was gone. I went to a doctor in

Beverly Hills, who swabbed some kind of oil on my throat and instantly my voice was fine.

But when I hit the sidewalk after I left the doctor, my voice was gone again. I went to another doctor at UCLA. After one look at my throat, he said, "You tell your doctor to put you in the hospital today. We operate tomorrow."

To say that I was frightened is putting it mildly. I was sure I was going to die.

The doctors took out a nodule that had grown inside my throat. It was benign, thank God. I lost about half my voice from that. I could still put out a pretty good holler, but after about two or three of them my voice would give out.

The famous Surgeon General's report had just come out, linking smoking to cancer. I didn't need the doctors to convince me to give up smoking. I still go to my doctor every year to look at my lungs, and they're still black from that awful cigarette smoke. He tells me they'll be that way for the rest of my life—a potential ticking time bomb.

So I beg you all, please: give up smoking. It's a drug, it's a nasty habit, and in the end it's going to kill you. If they could, I'm sure John Wayne, Lee Marvin, Yul Brynner, and some of the other colleagues of mine it's killed would agree.

The point of this long story is this: there are better ways to relax than by lighting a cigarette or getting drunk or doing drugs or any of the things we do to ourselves because of stress or social demands. And, you know, the time you sit there is not only relaxing, it's good for reflection. In our increasingly fast-paced world, I can't recommend that enough.

So here I am.

I've been knocking around this planet for nearly a century, working for much of that time and still raring to go.

Thanks to you, too, the fans who have stuck by me (and the readers who have stayed with me)! It's been a helluva journey, from Connecticut to Italy, from San Diego to Hawaii, from New York to Hollywood and all around the world.

The lifespan for an actor, Spencer Tracy once said, is about the same as that of the common housefly, although Mr. Tracy's incredible career belies that statement. My late friend Jack Elam once described the career of a character actor. It went like this: "Who's Jack Elam? Get me Jack Elam. Get me a Jack Elam type. Get me a young Jack Elam. Who's the hell's Jack Elam?"

While there's a lot of truth to that, the fact is, I've never had to consider retiring . I may not be as quick on my feet as I used to be. When I made *Aces and Eights* last year I needed a ladder to climb onto my horse. The guy helping me said, "Your ass used to be a lot younger." I said, "So was the horse." But I'm still in demand, still getting the calls.

Turns out I didn't win the Golden Globe for *A Grandpa for Christmas*, but that's okay. I've gone from a working stiff who didn't want to set the world on fire, who just wanted to keep his nuts warm, to where I am.

And that's been more than I could have ever hoped for.

God bless. And thanks for stopping by.

Acknowledgments

My dear wife Tova, whose diligence, Patience and love have kept me going for the thirty-five years that we have been married . . . so far. What else can I possibly say, except that she's the love of my life.

My dear associate, helper, and loyal lieutenant, Harry Flynn, whose constant urging helped me finish this book. Thanks to Jeff Rovin for smoothing it all out.

My dear friend George Lindsey.

My dear friend Andy Fenady, director, writer, producer, and the man who brought us to Citadel Press.

To all my old shipmates from the cast of *McHale's Navy*—and especially to Tim Conway, my comrade-in-arms on *SpongeBob SquarePants*.

There are so many people I've met over the years and whom I love dearly who, when they read this book, will know that they hold a special place in my heart.

Not last, not least, my associate Joyce McConnell, without whose patience, support, and work my last twenty-five years would have been a great deal tougher.

And thank you Gary Goldstein of Citadel Books. Your enthusiasm and helpfulness made it all happen.

Index

Printed in the United States
by Baker & Taylor Publisher Services